DOUBTING

Growing Through the Uncertainties of Faith

ALISTER MCGRATH

Foreword by Ravi Zacharias

IVP Books

An imprint of InterVarsity Press
Downers Grove, Illinois

InterVarsity Press
P.O. Box 1400, Downers Grove, IL 60515-1426
World Wide Web: www.ivpress.com
Email: email@ivpress.com

InterVarsity Press® is the book-publishing division of InterVarsity Christian Fellowship/USA®, a movement of students and faculty active on campus at hundreds of universities, colleges and schools of nursing in the United States of America, and a member movement of the International Fellowship of Evangelical Students. For information about local and regional activities, write Public Relations Dept., InterVarsity Christian Fellowship/ USA, 6400 Schroeder Rd., P.O. Box 7895, Madison, WI 53707-7895, or visit the IVCF website at <www.intervarsity.org>.

Scripture quotations, unless otherwise noted, are from the New Revised Standard Version of the Bible, copyright 1989 by the Division of Christian Education of the National Council of the Churches of Christ in the USA. Used by permission. All rights reserved.

Design: Cindy Kiple

Images: Storm clouds: © ninjaMonkeyStudio/iStockphoto
        Man in wheat field: MorganDDL/iStockphoto

ISBN 978-0-8308-3352-8

Printed in the United States of America ∞

Library of Congress Cataloging-in-Publication Data

McGrath, Alister E., 1953-
   Doubting: growing through the uncertainties of faith / Alister
McGrath.
      p. cm.
   Includes bibliographical references.
   ISBN-13: 978-0-8308-3352-8 (pbk.: alk. paper)
   ISBN-10: 0-8308-3352-8 (pbk.: alk. paper)
   1. Belief and doubt. 2. Faith. I. Title.
   BT774.M325 2006
   234'.23—dc22
                                                                    2006030475

P	21	20	19	18	17	16	15	14	13	12	11	10	9	8	7	6	5
Y	29	28	27	26	25	24	23	22	21	20	19	18	17	16	15	14

CONTENTS

FOREWORD

Some years ago I witnessed a criminal trial at the Old Bailey in London. The atmosphere was tense, filled with all of the attendant emotions—agony, anger and drama. It became very clear what the attorneys were seeking to do. They wanted to bring either certainty or doubt into the allegations, depending on the client they represented. All of us are familiar with such courtroom spectacles: opposing attorneys seek to discredit witnesses who injure their own case. The arguments move back and forth in an attempt by each side to gain the upper hand, and if the slightest doubt can be cast on the opponent, then somehow it is inferred that the whole weight of contrary testimony is false.

Such a maneuver is not difficult, and the end result is quite easy to accomplish. Indeed, this tactic has been the exact approach taken in the battle of ideas that has occupied center stage for centuries. The road taken from the Renaissance to the Enlightenment all the way to modernity and now postmodernity was, in hindsight, rather predictable. The hallmark of our education today is skepticism, going back to René Descartes' belief that the only thing we can be certain of is doubt. Only now, there is no God believed to respond to our uncertainties. We are alone with our doubts.

Rational certainty had always been that glittering dome, imagined or otherwise, on the huge edifice of philosophy. Descartes' starting point was *cogito ergo sum:* "I think, therefore I am." David Hume chiseled the statement down further and said we must eliminate the "I" to reach an even more fundamental assertion: "I think, therefore thinking exists." Hans Driesch, Danish biologist, went one better and said, "I am something (I can't be sure of what at this very moment when I raise this question)."

All this is reminiscent of the student at New York University who intimidatingly asked his professor, "Sir, how do I know that I exist?" A lingering pause preceded the professor's answer. He lowered his glasses, peered over the rim and riveted his eyes on the student. His simple response finally came, "And whom shall I say is asking?" Fortunately or otherwise, some things in life are just undeniable.

Further, as both Christian and postmodern philosophers have shown, it is impossible, when dealing with all of reality, to force mathematical certainty into every test for truthfulness. Life is just not livable that way, and in fact, science would collapse if it consistently believed that at every step. Einstein himself challenged this illusory certainty in mathematics, saying, "As far as the propositions of mathematics refer to reality, they are not certain; and as far as they are certain, they do not refer to reality." It would be better to describe our pursuit as that which seeks a high degree of certainty, or meaningful certainty.

As such, Alister McGrath rightly suggests that doubt is not something we can simply ascribe to determined skepticism or unbelief, but rather in part to our frailty as finite human beings. We are limited creatures—limited in power, knowledge and, yes, perspective. We do not see as we ought, and what we do see, we often doubt. Or, as the Scriptures attested nearly two millennia ago, "We see through a glass darkly."

In a Christmas Eve letter to friend Arthur Greeves, Oxford don C. S. Lewis admitted his own poignant struggle with doubt. Wrote Lewis,

> I think the trouble with me is *lack of faith*. I have no *rational* ground for going back on the arguments that convinced me of God's existence: but the irrational deadweight of my old sceptical habits, and the spirit of this age, and the cares of the day, steal away all my lively feeling of the truth, and often when I pray I wonder if I am not posting letters to a non-existent address. Mind you I don't *think* so—the whole of my reasonable mind is convinced: but I often *feel* so.

Likewise, Alister McGrath reveals and unravels the complexity of doubt with empathy and insight. Drawing on such authors as Lewis and Pascal, he writes that our doubting culture is also "a *longing* culture that knows it is searching for something that it has not yet found." And he continues, "There is so much that Christianity has to say here!"

In my own experience, after three decades of crisscrossing the globe and lecturing at numerous campuses around the world, I have witnessed this same spiritual yearning. Even in an age of uncertainty it is evident that these longings just will not completely die. In fact, in recent times virtually every engagement I have taken finds the auditorium filled to capacity. This is somewhat analogous to Russia and China—each in their way trying to exterminate God and finding out that he outlives his pallbearers. So it is in many of our universities too.

I am delighted to see this work from Alister who, with cogency and confidence, contends for the truth of the Christian message. His manner is winsome, his mind studied and his nature kind-hearted. Doubt is an invitation to growth and relationship, he tells us, and I trust as you read this book you will find his invitation to be genuine and convincing.

Ravi Zacharias
Author and speaker

PREFACE

I believe; help my unbelief!" (Mark 9:24). We don't know the name of the man who spoke these memorable words to Jesus. Whoever he was, his words capture perfectly the anxieties of many Christians. They have discovered in Jesus Christ something far more wonderful than they had ever dared to hope. God often seems very close in the first days of faith. Yet nagging doubts sometimes remain. Can I really trust in the gospel? Surely it's just too good to be true! Does God really love me? Can I be of any use to God? Deep down, many Christians worry about questions like these, often feeling ashamed for doing so. And so they suppress them. They hope that they will go away. Sometimes they do—but often they don't.

In this book I try to explain, as simply and clearly as possible, what doubt is and how it arises. We live in a culture that doubts everything as a matter of principle, often seeing commitment to any beliefs as the ultimate secular sin. Yet it is not enough to discuss doubt in such general terms. For this reason, I move on to deal with a series of very specific doubts and anxieties that many Christians experience, often in the first few years of their lives as believers. I offer some suggestions for handling doubt and for making your faith less vulnerable to it. Its main theme is simple: Doubt is an invitation to grow in faith and understanding, rather than something we need to panic about or get preoccupied with. We must all learn to grasp and value what Alfred, Lord Tennyson calls the "sunnier side of doubt."

This work had its origins in some talks given to students from Oxford University at a house party in December 1988. I rewrote it in December 2005 to take account of major cultural changes since that time, as well as my own deepened experience of engaging with the questions that trouble so many people. I hope that it will be a useful resource to those who experience doubt themselves, or would like to help their family and friends cope with its challenges.

Alister McGrath
Oxford University

1

DOUBT

What It Is—and What It Isn't

It's surprising how many Christians prefer not to talk about doubt. Some even refuse to think about it. Somehow, admitting to doubt seems to amount to insulting God, calling his integrity into question. It is quite understandable that you might feel this way about doubt: on the one hand, you may think that admitting to doubt is a sign of spiritual or intellectual weakness; on the other, you may be reluctant to admit those doubts to your friends, in case you upset them, perhaps damaging their own faith.

Many Christians thus suppress their doubts. They think that it is improper to own up to them. Or they are afraid that they will look stupid if they do. Maybe they are worried that their pride or self-esteem would suffer. Yet one of the reasons why so many Christians have difficulty in coping with doubt is that they confuse it with two quite separate ideas, which at first seem similar but are actually rather different.

In the first place, doubt is not *skepticism*—the decision to doubt everything deliberately, as a matter of principle.

In the second, it's not *unbelief*—the decision not to have faith in God. Unbelief is an act of will, rather than a difficulty in understanding. Sometimes we feel as if there is an "old Adam" within us, trying to sabotage our faith. We need help to overcome our old nature and its unbelieving outlook.

Doubt often means asking questions or voicing uncertainties from the standpoint of faith. You believe—but you have difficulties with that faith, or are worried about it in some way. Faith and doubt aren't mutually exclusive—but faith and unbelief are.

Doubt is probably a permanent feature of the Christian life. It's like some kind of spiritual growing pain. Sometimes it recedes into the background; at other times it comes to the forefront, making its presence felt with a vengeance. A medical practitioner I knew once remarked that life was a permanent battle against all sorts of diseases, with good health being little more than an ability to keep disease at bay. For some people the life of faith often seems like that—a permanent battle against doubt. It is helpful to think of doubt as a symptom of our human frailty, of our reluctance to trust God. Let's develop this by thinking about how people come to faith.

COMING TO FAITH—WITH UNRESOLVED DOUBTS

One way of understanding conversion runs like this: what stops people from coming to faith in God is doubt; after wrestling with these various doubts and overcoming them, the way is clear to come to faith. Coming to faith thus happens once all doubt has been cleared out of the way—faith excludes doubt!

Now it is quite possible that some people do come to faith this way. However, most do not. Experience suggests that a rather different way of understanding conversion is more reliable. Many people feel deeply attracted by the gospel, despite their doubts. On the one hand, their doubts are real and hold them back from faith; on the other, the pull of the gospel is very strong and draws them toward faith. In the end, they decide to put their trust in God and in Jesus Christ, despite unresolved anxieties and difficulties. They are still in two minds. They hope that their doubts and difficulties will be sorted out as they grow in faith. The seventeenth-century philosopher Francis Bacon commended this way in his *Advancement of Learning:* "If a man will begin with certainties, he will end in doubts; but if he is content to begin with doubts, he will end in certainties."

An analogy may make this clearer. Suppose you are at a really boring party one evening, when you meet someone you feel drawn to. You get to know this person and, as time goes on, realize you're falling in love. However, you hold back from allowing the relationship to develop any further. After all, you don't really know the other person that well. There might be some dark side to their character. Can you really trust them? And, like many people, you may have a sense of personal inadequacy: what, you wonder, could this other person possibly see in you? Could they ever possibly fall in love with you? You are profoundly attracted to them, yet you hold back. You have doubts. You're in two minds about it.

Now in this situation, you have two options. You can still hold back and become a prisoner of your doubts and hesitations. If we all did that all the time, we'd miss out on many of life's great adventures and surprises—including both falling in love and discovering the Christian faith. Or you can take a risk. You can say, "I'm going to give this a try, and hope that my doubts and anxieties will be resolved as things go on." And so you allow the relationship to develop.

Many people become Christians in that kind of spirit. They are aware of the enormous attraction of the gospel; they are deeply moved by the thought of Jesus Christ dying for their sins; they are excited by the great gospel promises of forgiveness and newness of life. Or they have experienced glimpses of transcendence and just *know* that there is a God out there. They decide to reach out in faith and claim these as their own. As for their doubts and anxieties? They hope that they will be resolved and put in their proper perspective as their relationship with God develops. "I believe; help my unbelief!" (Mark 9:24).

If you're in this situation, wrestling with doubt will be an important part of your life as a Christian. The way in which you came to faith sets an agenda for you. It decides what things need to be sorted out. You'll want to think about the same kinds of questions that arise in any personal relationship. Can I really trust God? Does he really love me? What about my personal inadequacies—does he know what I'm really like? And there may be other doubts about the gospel, about yourself, about Jesus Christ and about God himself. This book aims to deal with that agenda. But your doubts in no way invalidate your conversion experience—you really are a Christian!

DOUBT—A REMINDER OF HUMAN SINFULNESS AND FRAILTY

If we are going to set doubt in perspective, we need to see ourselves in the right perspective first. Above all, we need to appreciate the limits set on what we can know. We are finite, sinful human beings, and that limits what we can be sure about. In this section we will explore this theme in some detail.

The gospel is about redemption—about the transformation made possible by Christ, through the Spirit. We have been set free from sin through the death and resurrection of Jesus Christ. Redemption, however, is not something that can be achieved in an instant! The story is told of a little girl who asked a bishop whether he was saved. "I have been saved from the penalty of sin, I am being saved from the power of sin, and one day I shall be saved from the presence of sin," he replied. Salvation takes time! It is a process, in which we mature in faith, like a seed growing into a plant.

In classic evangelical thought, a useful distinction is made between justification and sanctification. In justification, we are declared to be right with God; our status changes, as we become an adopted child of God; we are given the gift of the Holy Spirit as a surety or pledge of being a Christian. Sanctification, however, is a long process, in which we are gradually conformed to the likeness of Christ. It cannot happen overnight. The fact that it takes so long does not point to any failing on God's part but indicates how deep-rooted sin is within us.

Martin Luther used a phrase that is very helpful here. He talked of the Christian as being "righteous and sinful at one and the same time." By this, Luther meant that Christians are righteous (in that we stand in a right relationship with God) but are still sinful (in that sin has yet to be completely eradicated from our nature). To use a military analogy, the decisive victory over sin has been achieved with your conversion; nevertheless, mopping up operations must continue, as isolated pockets of resistance are overcome. Sin may have been defeated in our lives; nevertheless, it remains a lingering presence. We are deluding ourselves if we pretend that we have no sin (1 John 1:8; 2:1). Ignoring sin, or pretending it's not there, points to an inadequate understanding of the seriousness of human sinfulness. For Paul, grace and sin are like two powers, battling it out within us. We know what the final outcome of that battle will be—but while it lasts, we cannot ignore its effects—*one of which is doubt.*

Doubt reflects the continued presence and power of sin within us, reminding us of our need for grace and preventing us from becoming complacent about our relationship with God. We are all sinners, and we all suffer from doubt, to a greater or lesser extent. Our relationship with God is something we need to work at, conscious that in doing so, we are working with God and not on our own (Philippians 2:12-13). Sin causes us to challenge the promises of God, to mistrust him. (Note how mistrust of God is the "original sin" of Genesis 3:1-5.) Only by causing us to turn away from God can sin regain its hold over us. Faith is not just a willingness and ability to trust in God—it is the channel through which God's grace flows to us. It is our lifeline to God. It is like the trunk of a tree, transferring life-giving sap from its roots to its branches—it both supports and nourishes their growth. Break that link, and the branches wither (cf. John 15:1-8). If sin has any strategy after your conversion, it is to break that link, to deny you access to the promises and power of God—and to allow itself to regain its former hold over your life.

Doubt, then, needs to be seen in its proper context—that of our struggle against sin (Hebrews 12:4). It is an integral part of the process of growing in faith and encountering resistance from our old natures in doing so.

Yet there is more to it than this. It is not entirely correct to describe doubt as simply due to human *sinfulness*. It is also a reflection of human *frailty*. We are human beings, and quite frankly, this means that we operate under limits. There are many things that we cannot do and many things that we cannot see—simply because we are human, not divine. We're like grasshoppers, trying to make sense of a vast universe (Isaiah 40:22). We're so small; how can we ever hope to make sense of something so immense? How can our tiny minds take in something so vast? That's why the idea of revelation is so important. If we were left to find out about God using our own limited resources, we wouldn't get very far. And God comes to our aid by making himself known. He takes the initiative.

The severe limitations placed on human capacities by the fact that we are creatures, not God, has been a major theme of Christian theology down through the centuries. God is bigger than we think—and our minds struggle even to begin to wrestle with him. Protesting against slick and too-easy notions of God in the fifth century, Augustine wrote of the inability of the human mind to comprehend God fully. If you can comprehend it, he remarked, it's not God. To comprehend is to grasp something in its totality. But what if it is too great, too deep, for us to do this? What if we are confronted with the deepest of oceans, and we can only skim its surface? If we cannot see something in its totality, we are not going to be able to make complete sense of it.

There is a story about Augustine worth telling here. Augustine is particularly remembered for a massive treatise he wrote on the mystery of the Trinity—the distinctively Christian understanding of the richly textured nature of God. Perhaps in the midst of writing this book, Augustine found himself pacing the Mediterranean shoreline of his native North Africa, not far from the great city of Carthage. While wandering across the sand, he noticed a small boy scooping seawater into his hands and pouring as much as his small hands could hold into a hole he had earlier hollowed in the sand. Puzzled, Augustine watched as the lad repeated his action again and again.

Eventually, his curiosity got the better of him. What, he asked the boy, did he think he was doing? The reply probably perplexed him still further. The boy informed him that he was in the process of emptying the ocean into the small cavity he had scooped out in the hot sand. Augustine laughed. How could such a vast body of water be contained in such a small hole? But the boy shot back his reply: how could Augustine expect to contain the vast mystery of God in the mere words of a book?

The story illuminates one of the central themes of Christian theology and spirituality alike—that there are limits placed on the human ability to grasp the things of God. And because we can't fully grasp something, we sometimes doubt that it is true. We misinterpret our inability to understand something as a sign that it is not true, or not real. In reality, the situation is very different. We are confronted with many things in the world—including the Christian gospel—that are just too big for our minds to embrace. And we have to learn to live with that tension—not doubting, but trusting.

Thomas Aquinas, writing in the thirteenth century, stressed that God was obliged to speak to us using images and analogies. Why? On account of the weakness of our intellects. Our minds aren't big enough to comprehend God. We cannot fully understand God and his ways; as a result, God reveals himself partially (but accurately and adequately), up to the limits of our abilities. This reflects a limitation on our part, not God's.

John Calvin, writing in the sixteenth century, set out a principle that is helpful here: "God accommodates himself to our weakness." In other words, God knows our limitations and adapts himself accordingly. We cannot see the full picture, so God presents us with a reliable guide to its contents, hitting the high points. No more is possible, given the limitations placed on us. Of course we have difficulties in trying to understand God and the world—but this doesn't mean that our faith is misplaced!

An example of how the limitations of being human affect the way we see things may help make this point clearer. Suppose you want to see the stars, or catch a glimpse of the Milky Way. You can't do this in broad daylight. You have to wait until it's dark. The stars are still there during the day; it's just that you can't see them. Our eyes just aren't discerning enough to pick up their light during the day. When it's night, our eyes adjust to allow us to see their tiny pinpoints of light, coming from the depths of our universe, highlighted against the blackness of the night. The stars don't need darkness to exist—but we need darkness if we are to see them and convince ourselves that they are still there!

So it is with God. Just as our eyes can't see stars during the day, so our minds can't take in the fullness of God. It's the way we see things, rather than the way things actually are, which is the problem here. (Or, to use the technical language of philosophy for a moment, the issue is *noetic,* not *ontic.*) Being human places limits on what we can see, know and understand.

We need to understand what those limits are because in the end, doubt arises partly on account of our unrealistic expectations about certainty. We think that we ought to be able to *prove* with absolute certainty that certain things are true—for example, that God exists. But it's just not like that. Being prepared to accept our limitations is an essential part of growing in faith. There's a paradox here: it's only when we use our reason that we begin to appreciate its limits. The great French writer and philosopher Blaise Pascal put this rather well in his *Pensées:* "Reason's final step is to realize that there are an infinite number of things which lie beyond it. It is simply feeble if it does not get as far as realizing that."

This principle applies to just about everything, not just to religious beliefs. In 1932 Albert Einstein wrote a letter to Queen Elizabeth of Belgium, in which he commented, "As a human being one has been endowed with intelligence to be able to see clearly how utterly inadequate that intelligence is when confronted with what exists." The point Einstein made is critically important. The world is something of a mystery, and the fact that we can make any kind of sense of it is something of a miracle. And there are limits to what we can understand, just as there are limits to what we can prove. And in such situations, we have to trust that we can get things more or less right.

It is only natural that we should want to see and know more. But that's overlooking our limitations. It's like saying, "Because I can't see the stars in the daylight, they're not really there." That's confusing our perception of the situation with the reality of that situation. The way we see things isn't necessarily the way things really are.

Doubt often reflects a sense of unease about the way in which experience, reason, feeling and faith relate. Sometimes they seem to be out of step with each other—so which do we believe? Which is right? The central insight here is that our frailty and weakness prevent us from fully comprehending the way in which these relate to each other. As the great Victorian preacher and novelist George MacDonald once pointed out, "Everything difficult indicates something more than our theory of life yet embraces." Faith assures us that, though we do not see the picture totally, we nevertheless see it reliably (1 Corinthians 13:12).

2

DOUBT AND THE VAIN SEARCH
FOR CERTAINTY

Deep within all of us lies a longing for absolute security, to be able to know with absolute certainty. We feel that we should be absolutely sure of everything that we believe. Surely, we feel, we ought to be able to prove everything that we believe?

Yet absolute certainty is actually reserved for a very small class of beliefs—for example, things that are self-evident or capable of being logically demonstrated by propositions. Christianity does not concern logical propositions or self-evident truths, such as 2 + 2 = 4, or "the whole is greater than the part." Both of these are certainly true, and we are able to know such truths with absolute certainty—but what is their relevance to life? Realizing that "the whole is greater than the part" isn't going to turn your life inside out! Knowing that two and two equal four isn't going to tell you anything much about the meaning of life. It won't excite you. Frankly, the sort of things that you can know with absolute certainty are actually not that important.

The things in life that really matter cannot be proven with certainty—whether they are ethical values (such as respect for human life), social attitudes (such as democracy) or religious beliefs (such

as Christianity). In his book *Democracy in America,* Alexis de
Tocqueville writes, "There is no philosopher in the world so great
but he believes a million things on the faith of other people and
accepts a great many more truths than he demonstrates." Richard
Rorty, probably the greatest American philosopher of the twentieth century, makes this point well in his book *The Consequences of
Pragmatism* when he points out that "if anyone really believed that
the worth of a theory depends on its philosophical grounding,
then indeed they would be dubious about physics, or democracy,
until relativism in respect to philosophical theories had been overcome. Fortunately, almost nobody believes anything of the sort."
His point? We can commit ourselves to the great worldviews of
our time without having to wait for absolute proof—a proof
which, by the very nature of things, is never going to happen.

The British nineteenth-century poet Alfred, Lord Tennyson
made this point rather nicely in his poem "The Ancient Sage":

> For nothing worthy proving can be proven,
> Nor yet disproven; wherefore thou be wise,
> Cleave ever to the sunnier side of doubt.

The beliefs that are really important in life concern such things
as whether there is a God and what he is like, or the mystery of
human nature and destiny. These—and a whole host of other important beliefs—have two basic features. In the first place, they are
relevant to life. They matter, in that they affect the way we think,
live, hope and act. In the second place, by their very nature they
make claims that *cannot be proved* (or disproved) with total certainty. At best we may hope to know them as probably true. There
will always be an element of doubt in any statement that goes beyond the world of logic and self-evident propositions. Christianity

is not unique in this respect: an atheist or Marxist is confronted with precisely the same dilemma. Anyone who wants to talk about the meaning of life has to make statements that rest on faith, not absolute certainty. Anyway, God isn't a proposition—he's a person!

We cannot see God; we cannot touch him; we cannot demand that he give a public demonstration of his existence or character. We know of God only through faith. Yet the human mind wants more. "Give us a sign! Prove it!" It is an age-old problem. Those who heard Jesus' teaching wanted a sign (Matthew 12:38)—something which would confirm his authority, which would convince them beyond any doubt.

To believe in God demands an act of faith—as does the decision not to believe in him. Neither is based on absolute certainty, nor can it be. To accept Jesus demands a leap of faith—but so does the decision to reject him. To accept Christianity demands faith—and so does the decision to reject it. Both rest on faith, in that nobody can prove with absolute certainty that Jesus is the Son of God, the risen Savior of humanity—just as nobody can prove with absolute certainty that he is not. The decision, whatever it may be, rests on faith. There is an element of doubt in each case. Every attitude toward Jesus—except the decision not to have any attitude at all!—rests on faith, not certainty. *Faith is not belief without proof but trust without reservations—trust in a God who has shown himself worthy of that trust.* To use a trinitarian framework: God the Father makes those promises; God the Son confirms them in his words and deeds; and the Holy Spirit reassures us of their reliability and seals those promises within our hearts.

These points are reflected in the American writer Sheldon Vanauken's account, in his book *A Severe Mercy,* of his mental wrestling before his conversion at Oxford. He found himself caught in a dilemma over the role of proof in faith, which many others have experienced.

There is a gap between the probable and the proved. How was I to cross it? If I were to stake my whole life on the risen Christ, I wanted proof. I wanted certainty. I wanted to see him eat a bit of fish. I wanted letters of fire across the sky. I got none of these. . . . It was a question of whether I was to accept him—or reject. My God! There was a gap behind me as well! Perhaps the leap to acceptance was a horrifying gamble—but what of the leap to rejection? There might be no certainty that Christ was God—but, by God, there was no certainty that he was not. This was not to be borne. I could not reject Jesus. There was only one thing to do once I had seen the gap behind me. I turned away from it, and flung myself over the gap towards Jesus.

There is indeed a leap of faith involved in Christianity—but it is not an irrational leap into the dark. The Christian experience is that of being caught safely by a loving and living God, whose arms await us as we leap. Martin Luther put this rather well: "Faith is a free surrender and a joyous wager on the unseen, untried and unknown goodness of God."

All outlooks on life, all theories of the meaning of human existence, rest on faith, in that they cannot be proved with absolute certainty. But this doesn't mean that they're all equally probable or plausible! Let's take three theories of the significance of Jesus to illustrate this point.

1. We have been redeemed from sin by the death and resurrection of Jesus Christ.

2. Jesus and his disciples were actually the advance guard of

a Martian invasion force, who mistook Earth for the planet Venus on account of a navigation error.

3. Jesus was not really a person but a hallucinogenic mushroom.

Although none of these can be proved or disproved with absolute certainty, it will be obvious that they cannot all be taken with quite the same degree of seriousness!

Let's be quite clear: Nobody can prove Christianity with total certainty. But that's not really a problem. The big questions concern the reliability of its historical foundations, its internal consistency, its rationality, its power to convert and its relevance to human existence. As C. S. Lewis stressed in *Mere Christianity*, Christianity has exceptionally fine credentials on all counts. Look into them. You can totally commit yourself to the gospel in full confidence, as a powerful, credible and profoundly satisfying answer to the mystery of human existence. Faith is basically the resolve to live our lives on the assumption that certain things are true and trustworthy, in the confident assurance that they are true and trustworthy, and that one day we will know with absolute certainty that they are true and trustworthy.

A SUPERFICIAL FAITH IS A VULNERABLE FAITH

Superficiality is a curse of our age. The demand for instant satisfaction leads to superficial personal relationships and a superficial Christian faith. Many students discover Christianity for the first time while in college. This discovery very often happens alongside other important events like leaving the parental home, falling in love or gaining independence of thought and action. As a result, initial emphasis very often falls on the emotional and experiential aspects of Christianity. There is nothing wrong with this! Christianity has abundant resources for those who wish to place emphasis on the role of experience in the life of faith. But there is more to faith than that.

Faith has three main elements. In the first place, it is *trust* in God. It is a confidence in the trustworthiness, fidelity and reliability of God. It is about rejoicing in his presence and power, being open to his prompting and guidance through prayer, and experiencing the motivation and comfort of the Holy Spirit. It is a deep sense of longing to be close to God, of wanting to praise him, of being aware of his presence. In many ways this aspect of Christian faith is like being in love with someone: you want to be with them, enjoying their presence and feeling secure with them. It concerns the heart rather than the head; it is emotional rather than intellectual. It is the powerhouse of Christian life, keeping us going through the difficult times and exciting us during the good times.

The difficulty is that all too many people seem to get no further than this stage. Their faith can easily become nothing more than emotion. It can become superficial, lacking any real depth, not really having taken root and not being very vulnerable. Yet there is more to faith than emotion, experience and feelings, however important they may be. Faith can only flourish when it sinks deep roots. Christianity isn't just about experiencing God—it's about sticking to God. A mature faith is something secure, something that you can rely on. If your faith is not deeply rooted, you will be tempted to find security in something else, only to find that this alternative will fail you (Matthew 7:24-27).

In the second place, faith is *understanding* more about God, Jesus Christ, and human nature and destiny. By its very nature, faith seeks understanding. It seeks to take root in our minds, as we think through the implications of our experience of the risen Christ. To become a Christian is to encounter and embrace the reality of God; to become a disciple is to allow this encounter to shape the way we think—and act.

In the third place, faith is *obedience.* Paul speaks of the "obedience that comes from faith" (Romans 1:5), making the point that faith must express itself in the way we act. British essayist Joseph Addison says, "Faith is kept alive in us, and gathers strength, from practice more than speculation." Or, as the Oxford writer W. H. Griffith-Thomas links them in his book *The Principles of Theology:*

> [Faith] commences with the conviction of the mind based on adequate evidence; it continues in the confidence of the heart or emotions based on conviction, and it is crowned in the consent of the will, by means of which the conviction and confidence are expressed in conduct.

And it's at this point that doubt can come in, simply when faith is allowed to be shallow. The New Testament often compares faith to a growing plant—a very helpful model. It is easy to uproot a plant in its early stages of growth; once it has laid down roots, however, it is much harder to dislodge it. By failing to allow their faith to take root by seriously thinking about their faith, some Christians make themselves vulnerable to doubt. For example, someone may raise a question about the historical evidence for the existence of Jesus. They don't know the answer. So doubts begin to creep in—often quite needless doubts, it must be said.

If this happens to you, view it in the right way. The gospel isn't an illusion that is shown for what it really is by hard questions—like the emperor's clothes in the famous story by Hans Christian Andersen. The fact that you haven't been able to give adequate answers to some person's questions or objections to your faith doesn't mean that Christianity falls to pieces the moment people start asking hard questions! It doesn't mean that you've committed some kind of intellectual suicide by becoming a Christian. It shouldn't mean that your confidence and trust in the gospel collapse, like a deflating balloon, just because someone asked you a question you couldn't answer. It does, however, mean that you might not have thought these things through.

Your faith is real—but may not be mature. It may be a little shallow and superficial. But—and this matters enormously—*faith can grow*, and it strengthens as it grows. It needs to take root and grow into a strong, vibrant plant. The problem lies not in the gospel but in the nature and depth of your response to it. You may have allowed the gospel to capture your imagination but not your mind. Your faith may be shallow when it should be—and can be—profound. Failure here ought to challenge you to go away and read more deeply about these matters, or talk them over with other more experienced Christians. In addition to helping you deepen your understanding of these things, doing this will enable you to be more helpful to those interested in learning about Christianity.

This doesn't mean that you should try harder to believe, as if it were by wishing harder that difficulties would disappear. This idea of "faith in faith" won't get you very far. You should see doubt as pointing to your faith possibly being based on weak foundations. It is those foundations that need attention. A superficial faith is a vulnerable faith, easily (and needlessly) upset when confronted with questions or criticism.

Faith is like reinforced concrete. Concrete that is reinforced with a steel framework is able to stand far greater stress and strain than concrete on its own. Experience that is reinforced with understanding will not crumble easily under pressure. Faith is like the flesh and bones of a human body. Just as the human skeleton supports the flesh, giving it shape and strength, so understanding supports and gives shape to Christian experience. Without the skeleton, the human body would collapse into a floppy mass. Without flesh, a skeleton is lifeless, hollow and empty. Both flesh and bones are needed if the body is to grow and function properly. Faith needs the vitality of experience if it is to live—and the support of understanding if it is to survive. So reinforce your faith with understanding.

3

DOUBT IN OTHER WORLDVIEWS

The Case of Atheism

In the previous chapter, I made an important point that needs to be explored much more thoroughly. Christians tend to think that doubt is a problem for them alone. But it's not. It's a problem for any worldview—whether Jewish or Islamic, atheist or religious. Appreciating this point is essential to seeing doubt in its proper perspective. As I used to be an atheist myself, I am going to explore the place of doubt within atheism.

Most people—including, it has to be said, many atheists themselves!—have the rather simple idea that atheism is about fact, whereas Christianity is about faith. Their ideas are factual; those of Christians are unproven. But it's not like that. Let me explain by asking a question: can I prove with certainty that there is a God? The short answer is no. If you have time to study the history of the philosophical arguments for the existence of God, you'll know that they are suggestive but not conclusive. It's pretty much the universal consensus within philosophy that rational argument does not settle the question of God's existence, one way or the other. The atheist philosopher Kai Nielsen makes this point clearly when he writes in his book *Reason and Practice*: "To show that an argument is invalid or unsound is not to show that the conclusion of the argument is false. . . . All the proofs of God's existence may fail, but it still may be the case that God exists." Argument is not going to settle this question one way or the other. And that means that the outcome is uncertain for the atheist.

Now let's pause here, because we need to appreciate something important. Christians often tend to see only one side of that statement—that nobody can rationally prove that God *exists*. But there is another side to it—nobody can *disprove* that God exists. Christians who believe in God do so as a matter of faith. But atheists have to do the same; their belief that there is no God is exactly that—a *belief*. Because they cannot prove that there is no God, their atheism is also a faith.

Atheists don't like this argument, but it is correct. The simple fact is that when *anyone* starts making statements about the meaning of life, the existence of God or whether there is life after death, they are making statements of faith. You can't prove, either by rational argument or by scientific investigation, what life is all about. Whether you are Christian or atheist, you share the same problem. It's essential that we appreciate that it's not just Christians that make these statements as a matter of faith. Because we all make these statements as a matter of faith, we are just as vulnerable to doubt as anyone else—Christians included. We're all in the same situation.

Let's explore this a little further by looking at two important issues: atheist arguments for the nonexistence of God and so-called scientific atheism, which holds that science disproves God's existence. Both, as we'll discover, are hopeless overstatements of the real situation.

ATHEIST ARGUMENTS AGAINST THE EXISTENCE OF GOD

Atheists often tell Christians that their faith is infantile. It's just fine for the minds of impressionable young children, but it's laughable in the case of adults. We've grown up now and need to move on. Why should we believe things that can't be scientifically proved? Faith in God, many atheists argue, is just like believing in Santa Claus and the tooth fairy. When you grow up, you grow out of it. And if you don't, then you are either mentally retarded or intellectually dishonest.

But this is just rhetoric: the attempt to discredit a belief by heaping ridicule on it. In fact, it is this argument itself that is childish. I stopped believing in Santa Claus and the tooth fairy when I was about six years old. After being an atheist for some years, I discovered God when I was eighteen and have never regarded this as some kind of infantile regression. As I noticed while researching my book *The Twilight of Atheism,* a large number of people come to believe in God in later life—when they are "grown up." I have yet to meet anyone who came to believe in Santa Claus or the tooth fairy late in life! So let's look at a more serious argument often advanced by atheists.

The most sophisticated atheistic arguments against God date from the nineteenth and early twentieth centuries, and they are found in the writings of Ludwig Feuerbach, Karl Marx and Sigmund Freud. Although they are slightly different, there is a common structure to each. Here it is, set out step by step:

1. There is no God.

2. But some people believe in God.

3. Since there is no God, this must be the result of some kind

of delusion or wishful thinking.

4. People believe in God because they want to. Their faith is just a wish-fulfillment.

5. So faith in God is just a human invention, corresponding to a human need. (Atheists differ over how this need arises: Marx puts it down to social alienation, Freud to psychological forces.)

The faith of atheists often rests heavily on this kind of argument, as I have found out in university debates. But let's look at this argument in more detail. On closer examination, it turns out to be as full of holes as Swiss cheese. There are three major points that need to be made.

1. The argument is circular. It presupposes that there is no God. Step 5 depends on step 1. If there was a God, then there would be no delusion, would there? It proves nothing except that atheism is logically self-sufficient. And so is just about every worldview. The important question is: how well does it relate to the real world? The argument merely restates its presuppositions as its conclusions.

2. It is logically flawed. It is certainly true that nothing exists just because I want it to. I might long to have a pile of hundred dollar bills beside me so that I could pay off some of my debts. But wanting something doesn't make it happen! We can all agree on that, I think. But—and this is a very big but—it does not follow that simply because I want something, that something cannot exist. Imagine a man who has fallen overboard from a ship. He wants there to be a helicopter to rescue him. So helicopters can't exist because he wants them to? Or the specific helicopter that is already on its way to rescue him cannot exist because he needs it? Or imagine that you feel very thirsty. You need a drink of water. So water can't exist because you want it? Or the specific glass of water that you are about to drink cannot exist because you need it just then? It just doesn't follow. As C. S. Lewis so often pointed out, it looks as if God has made us in such a way that we long for him—and then go on to find him! The desire for God originates from God—and eventually leads to God!

3. The argument works just as well against atheism. The atheist's argument goes like this: you want there to be a God. So you invent him. Your religious views are invented to correspond to what you want. But this line of argument works just as well against atheism. Imagine an extermination camp commandant during the Second World War. Would there not be excellent reasons for supposing that he might hope that God does *not* exist, given what might await him on the day of judgment? And might not his atheism itself be a wish-fulfillment? This is a devastating point. As cultural historians have pointed out for many years, based on their analysis of European history from about 1780 to 1980, people often reject the idea of God because they long for autonomy—the right to do what they please, without any interference from God. They don't need to worry about divine judgment; they reject belief in God because it suits them. That's what they want, but that doesn't mean that this is the way things really are.

This point was made superbly by the Polish philosopher and writer Czeslaw Milosz, who won the Nobel Prize for literature in 1980. Parodying the old Marxist idea that religion was the "opium of the people," he remarks in *The Discreet Charm of Nihilism* that a new opium has taken its place: rejection of belief in God on account of its implications for our ultimate accountability. "A true opium of the people is a belief in nothingness after death—the huge solace of thinking that for our betrayals, greed, cowardice, murders we are not going to be judged."

Atheism thus depends on a core belief that it cannot verify. Do you see the importance of this point? Atheists live out their lives on the basis of the belief that there is no God, believing that this is right but not being able to prove it conclusively. Hardly surprising, atheists have tried to buttress their beliefs in other ways. One of them is to appeal to the natural sciences. These, we are told with great confidence by atheists, have disproved belief in God. But is this really the case?

THE INCONCLUSIVE CASE OF SCIENTIFIC ATHEISM

The twentieth century has seen many atheist scientists insist that science has eliminated belief in God. The Oxford zoologist and atheist propagandist Richard Dawkins is a good example of this kind of writer. His simplistic overstatements are regularly criticized by other scientists as representing a serious abuse of the scientific method. The simple truth is that the natural sciences neither prove nor disprove the existence of God. So either we have to give up this discussion as meaningless, or we settle it on other grounds.

You will have no problem finding writers who talk about the "limitless powers of science" to explain things or who argue that only scientific knowledge can be taken seriously. Here is the British atheist writer Bertrand Russell, from his *Religion and Science*, on this point: "Whatever knowledge is attainable, must be attained by scientific methods; and what science cannot discover, mankind cannot know." Yet this is a ludicrous overstatement. First, it is not actually a scientific statement, so it disqualifies itself as being true knowledge! Yet more seriously, it would mean that we can never answer questions about the meaning of life, even from an atheist perspective—something that Russell seems to overlook.

Science has its limits. That's no criticism of science, by the way—just a recognition of its boundaries. Within those boundaries, it is highly competent. But outside them, it cannot deliver the simple answers that some hoped for. Sir Peter Medawar, who won a Nobel Prize for medicine for his discovery of acquired immunological tolerance, was well aware of the limits of science. His words from *The Limits of Science* deserve to be pondered:

> The existence of a limit to science is, however, made clear by its inability to answer childlike elementary questions having to do with first and last things—questions such as "How did everything begin?"; "What are we all here for?"; "What is the point of living?"

The point is clear: science is wonderful when it comes to discovering the chemical structure of planetary atmospheres, determining the cause of cancer or finding a cure for blood poisoning. But can it tell us why we are here? Or whether there is a God or not? No. It has its limits. And those who insist—quite wrongly—that science *demands* or *necessitates* or *proves* atheism have some serious explaining to do. Let's hear Sir Peter again:

> There is no quicker way for a scientist to bring discredit upon himself and upon his profession than roundly to declare—particularly when no declaration of any kind is called for—that science knows, or soon will know, the answers to all questions worth asking, and that questions which do not admit a scientific answer are in some way non-questions or "pseudo-questions" that only simpletons ask and only the gullible profess to be able to answer.

Let's be clear about this. It is perfectly possible to *interpret* the natural sciences in atheistic, theistic and agnostic ways. The sciences can be spun in ways making them support disbelief in God, belief in God or skepticism. But the sciences *demand* none of these interpretations. Stephen Jay Gould, widely regarded as America's greatest evolutionary biologist before his recent death from cancer, was no religious believer. But he was adamant that his own religious skepticism could not be derived from the sciences. As he wrote in *Darwin's Revolution in Thought:*

> To say it for all my colleagues and for the umpteenth million time (from college bull sessions to learned treatises): science simply cannot (by its legitimate methods) adjudicate the issue of God's possible superintendence of nature. We neither affirm nor deny it; we simply can't comment on it as scientists.

Gould rightly insists that science can work only with naturalistic explanations; it can neither affirm nor deny the existence of God. And those who argue that it disproves God have just lost the plot, imposing their atheism on a neutral science.

God is simply not an empirical hypothesis that can be checked out by the scientific method. As Stephen Jay Gould and others have insisted, the natural sciences are not capable of adjudicating, negatively or positively, on the God-question. It lies beyond their legitimate scope. There is simply no logically watertight means of arguing from observation of the world to the existence or nonexistence of God. This has not stopped people from doing so, as a casual survey of writings on both sides of the question indicates. But it does mean that these "arguments" are suggestive and nothing more. The grand idea that atheism is the only option for a thinking person has long since passed away, being displaced by a growing awareness of the limitations placed on human knowledge, and an increased expectation of humility in the advocation of religious choices.

Two major surveys of the religious beliefs of scientists, carried out at the beginning and end of the twentieth century, bear witness to a highly significant trend. One of the most widely held beliefs within atheist circles has been that, as the beliefs and practices of the "scientific" worldview became increasingly accepted within Western culture, the number of practicing scientists with any form of religious beliefs would dwindle to the point of insignificance. A survey of the religious views of scientists, undertaken in 1916, showed that about 40 percent of scientists had some form of personal religious beliefs. At the time, this was regarded as shocking, even scandalous. The survey was repeated in 1996 and showed no significant reduction in the proportion of scientists holding such beliefs, seriously challenging the popular notion of the relentless erosion of religious faith within the profession. The survey cuts the ground from under those who argued that the natural sciences are necessarily atheistic. Forty percent of those questioned had active religious beliefs, 40 percent had none (and can thus legitimately be regarded as atheist) and 20 percent were agnostic.

The stereotype of the necessarily atheist scientist lingers on in Western culture at the dawn of the third millennium. It has its uses and continues to surface in the rehashed myths of the intellectual superiority of atheism over its rivals. The truth, as might be expected, is far more complex and considerably more interesting.

The point of these reflections is obvious. *Any* worldview—atheist, Islamic, Jewish, Christian or whatever—ultimately depends on assumptions that cannot be proved. Every house is built on foundations, and the foundations of worldviews are not ultimately capable of being proved in every respect. Everyone who believes anything significant or worthwhile about the meaning of life does so *as a matter of faith.* We're all in the same boat. And once you realize this, doubt seems a very different matter. It's not a specifically Christian problem—it's a universal human problem. And that helps to set it in its proper perspective.

4

THE PERSONAL ASPECTS OF DOUBT

We're all different. People sometimes talk about different "personalities" or "personality types." This can be helpful, up to a point; for example, some people place emphasis on understanding, while others place that emphasis on experiencing. The idea of a "personality," however, suggests that individuals are static, and it doesn't pay enough attention to the fact that we change and develop in response to situations. What we are like is affected by the situations we've been through. Part of the reason that we're all different is that we've been through different situations. Who you are and the experiences you've been through can have a quite definite effect on the anxieties and doubts you have in relation to your Christian faith. Some examples will help make this point clearer.

Ann had a very difficult relationship with her father in her youth as a result of her mother's early death. Her memories of her father are dominated by his tyranny and insensitivity. She cannot remember her father ever doing anything to make her believe that he loved her. She looks back to the day when she left home to go to college as a moment of liberation, when she was able to break free from his oppressive presence. The word *father* has, as a result, only negative associations. Ann has considerable personal difficulties with thinking of God as a father and has real doubts about whether God can be said to love her.

Bill has a track record of persistent failure, both in academic studies and personal relationships. His family places considerable emphasis on success and the achievement of status, and they have made it clear that they regard him as something of a disappointment. He hasn't met the standards of his high-achieving parents. As a result, he has now acquired a deeply ingrained sense of failure and personal inability. Bill finds the gospel intimidating because it seems to make demands that he thinks he cannot meet. He is frightened of failing God. He has genuine and deep doubts and anxieties about whether he can ever really be a Christian.

Clare has been through a series of broken personal relationships, which have left her feeling deeply hurt. Her rather bitter experience of life has persuaded her that people cannot be trusted. She has experienced exploitation and abuse in relationships. She is now very reluctant to get involved in any further personal commitments, as she fears the results. Her experience of relationships leads her to believe that she only makes herself vulnerable and weak through trusting others and allowing herself to become close to them. Consequently, she finds it difficult to commit herself to God. She feels he cannot be trusted. She is very reluctant to get involved in a relationship with him.

Many more examples could be given. But the basic idea is clear: your background can affect your faith. The situations you've been through in the past may cause you anxieties relating to your faith. Your past may predispose you to certain doubts, anxieties and worries. In other words, present doubts may well reflect the continuing influence of past situations. Many people find it useful to try and identify the way in which their past affects their present, especially if this influence is unhelpful. You might like to try doing this with a sympathetic friend or counselor.

However, the main point to be made here is simple: our doubts, anxieties and difficulties often reflect our individuality. You may see things in a different way from your friends, simply because you are who you are. You may worry about something that doesn't bother your best friend at all. You may find it difficult to understand why your best friend has problems where you have none. In part, this may just reflect the fact that you and your best friend are different people who have been through and been affected by different situations. Our doubts often mirror our situation and help us realize more about ourselves. If you want to help someone with difficulties or anxieties about their faith, you may find you need to understand them as individuals before you can be much help. You may find that you can't give the same textbook answer to them all. So be sensitive to your own individuality and that of others. It may affect your faith—and your doubts.

Let's think about this a little more. Some people find it difficult to accept that God loves them. The reasons for their difficulties often reflect their background and the values instilled into them by their families. For example, they might be perfectionists who feel that they must do something or achieve something before God can love them. For this sort of person, the gospel proclamation of the unconditionality of God's love for us can be difficult to accept—it contradicts the standards of the world. Or they may have been taught that dependency is to be discouraged. Some individuals believe strongly in the cult of independence: personal fulfillment is based on not being dependent on anyone or anything. The idea that God loves us is an invitation to learn to depend on God. This clashes with the set of values they have been taught by their families, who are anxious that they should get ahead in the world through being independent. In both these cases, it is necessary to question how appropriate these values are and whether they apply to our relationship with God. But the basic point remains the same: your past history can affect the way you react to the gospel and the difficulties you experience in relation to it. Faith is a relational matter.

"DOUBTING IT" AND "DOUBTING YOU"

The word *doubt* can have two slightly different meanings. We could call these cognitive, which doubts statements, and personal, which doubts persons. One is a *doubt-it*, the other a *doubt-you* problem. One is fundamentally *intellectual;* the other is basically *relational.* Let's begin by looking at a doubt-it situation.

The New Testament provides us with an excellent illustration of this kind of doubt. After the resurrection, Jesus appeared to his disciples in the upper room. They were both surprised and overjoyed (John 20:19-20). However, one of the disciples, Thomas, wasn't there on that occasion. He missed the experience the others had of the presence of the risen Christ. And when they told him about it, he found it rather difficult to accept. "Unless I see the mark of the nails in his hands, and put my finger in the mark of the nails and my hand in his side, I will not believe" (John 20:25). Thomas doubted the belief of the remaining disciples that Jesus had been raised. That doubt was resolved through his encounter with the risen Christ, who spoke these words: "Do not doubt but believe" (John 20:27).

The second type of doubt is slightly different. Thomas doubted *something;* you can also doubt *someone.* It's a doubt-*you,* not a doubt-*it,* situation. To doubt someone is not to trust them, to have difficulty taking them at their word. Suppose I lent a colleague a large sum of money. He had promised to repay me, but it never happened. If he was to ask me to lend him some more money, I think I would hesitate before doing so! I would doubt his word. I would not have faith in his promises. My colleague *exists*—but that's not the issue here. I'm not doubting whether he really is there; my worries are about whether I can really trust him.

Someone may have profound difficulties trusting God as a person because of their past experiences. They may be reluctant to commit themselves, on account of their past experience of the untrustworthiness of people in relationships. They may not doubt that God exists; they do, however, doubt him as a person. Can God really be trusted, they wonder? Does he keep his promises? Does he really love us? That sort of doubt can cast so deep a shadow that everything else seems of little importance. Why worry about doubts or difficulties concerning Christian beliefs, when God may not be worth believing in? Why bother about problems of Christian faith, if you are hesitant about committing yourself to God in the first place? This is a doubt-you problem.

The gospel centers on the absolute trustworthiness, goodness and faithfulness of God as we know him and see him revealed in Jesus Christ. Therefore, I will move on to deal with some questions touching on the trustworthiness of God himself, in the hope that this may help people with such anxieties.

There are obvious connections between doubt and faith. I can believe that certain things are true, just as I can doubt that they are true. In part, this reflects the nature of the gospel itself. The gospel declares that certain things are true, for example, that Jesus really did rise from the dead (1 Corinthians 15:3-5). It also makes some crucial affirmations about God himself. God is trustworthy; he is faithful (Romans 3:3; 1 Thessalonians 5:24). To doubt God is to question his faithfulness and reliability. If we trust the *statement* that Jesus rose from the dead, we can trust the *person* of God. One of the reasons why we can trust God is that he raised Jesus from the dead; this shows that he is faithful to his promises. It is, however, helpful to make this distinction between two aspects of doubt and faith at this early stage. I will return to the question of trusting God later in this work.

It is important, however, to appreciate that doubts concern more than God. Many Christians have doubts about themselves (perhaps reflecting their background and personal history), which spill over into their thinking about God. For this reason, I have tried to bring together in this book some of the more common doubts Christians have and have grouped them together roughly in four categories: doubts about the gospel, about ourselves, about Jesus and about God. But before we go further, we need to look at the idea of doubt more closely.

5

DOUBT IN THE BIBLE

Analogies and Images

The New Testament doesn't use one single word throughout to represent *doubt*. Rather, it uses a range of words, each of which illuminates one particular aspect of what doubt really is. Each is like a snapshot of a landscape or a building: it's not good enough in itself to give a total picture, but it can give an excellent idea of what one aspect is like. And a series of snapshots builds up to give a total picture.

BIBLICAL IMAGES OF DOUBT

There are four main images used in the New Testament, each of which illuminates one angle of the concept of doubt.

Hesitation. After his resurrection, Jesus appeared on a mountain to his disciples. Matthew describes the scene thus: "When they saw him, they worshiped him; but some doubted" (Matthew 28:17). Although all the disciples encountered the risen Christ, some clearly had difficulty accepting what had happened. Perhaps they felt that it was too good to be true. Perhaps they were frightened and shocked by what happened. The Greek word used here (*distazo*) has the sense of "to hold back" or "to hesitate."

The same word (and the same idea) may be found earlier in Matthew's Gospel (Matthew 14:31), in the description of the storm at sea. Here, Peter's lack of faith is shown in his hesitation to put his trust in Jesus. Hesitation betrays a lack of trust. If you hesitate to accept an offer, it's because you have misgivings about it. You may not trust the person who is making the offer. You may not understand what it implies. You suspect that there may be something wrong with it. Our reluctance to accept the gospel wholeheartedly, with the enthusiasm of little children, reflects a basic lack of trust in God and his promises. We hesitate to accept them. We hold back.

Indecision. In stressing the importance of faith to the individual believer, Jesus points out the need not to doubt (Matthew 21:21). Paul notes how Abraham trusted in God's promise: "No distrust made him waver concerning the promise of God, but he grew strong in his faith as he gave glory to God" (Romans 4:20). The Greek word used here (*diakrino*) originally had the sense of "argue with," "to be at odds with," or "take issue with." This older meaning can still be seen in Acts 11:2, describing how Peter found himself in disputation with Jewish sympathizers in Jerusalem. However, in the New Testament a more subtle, developed meaning can be seen—to argue *with yourself*. The word now refers to an internal mental debate reflecting indecision and a lack of conviction. The same idea and word is used in James 1:6, with a powerful image— a wave tossed by the wind in a stormy sea—which we will explore further in a moment. You are divided within yourself, unsure of what to do.

In his letters, Paul frequently speaks of having "put off your old self" once becoming a Christian (Romans 6:6; Ephesians 4:22; Colossians 3:9). Part of the problem that many of us have is that our former unconverted self seems to live on! It is almost as if there is a debate going on between the old self and the new self. The former is highly skeptical of God's promises, while the latter wants to embrace them wholeheartedly. The result? Indecision. Hesitation. Wavering. Lack of confidence in God. The very existence of doubt reminds us of how easy it is not to allow God into every part of our lives. We are reluctant to allow God to take control of us. It is as if we have opened the door of our life to the risen Christ (Revelation 3:20) but only allowed him a toehold in our home. We are reluctant to admit him fully. We treat him like a guest, when we ought to be treating him as the Lord. Doubt may thus be a symptom of our lack of commitment to God.

Doubt is a way in which God is able to deepen our faith by showing us our lack of faith. The existence of doubt is like a signpost, showing us how far we have to go before we have fully committed ourselves to God. It shows as sheer illusion any temptation we may have to rely on ourselves rather than God. It is, therefore, with a sense of relief that we read Paul's words (Romans 3:3-4), reminding us that our lack of faith in no way alters God's faithfulness toward us! We can always turn to him in prayer and ask him to help our unbelief. Like the man who came to Jesus, we can pray: "I believe; help my unbelief!" (Mark 9:24).

Being in two minds. Doubters are described as "doubleminded" (*dipsychos*) in James 4:8. To doubt is to be in two minds about something. It implies indecision, hesitation and a resulting lack of progress. When I studied medieval philosophy at the university, I remember being intrigued by the problem known as "Buridan's Ass." (Actually, the medieval philosopher John Buridan really tells the story about a dog, not an ass.) Suppose you have a hungry donkey placed midway between two piles of food. If it's going to survive, it will need to make a decision to eat one of them. But what happens if it can't make up its mind? In the end the unfortunate donkey dies, having been unable to make a decision about which pile of food to eat.

There's an obvious parallel here with doubt. We are confronted with two different options: to believe or not to believe. It is very difficult to postpone a decision on this one. Each has its own very different rewards. Yet those rewards are only gained by commitment. For example, it would be very difficult for someone to adopt an "eat, drink and be merry for tomorrow we die" attitude to life, if he half-believes in the resurrection and future divine judgment. Likewise, it would be difficult for a Christian to take the great gospel promises of resurrection and eternal life seriously, if he half believes that there is nothing after death. Each of these individuals is in two minds; they have a foot in each camp. People like that are in the same position as Buridan's ass—they can't fully benefit from either pile of food.

Doubt means not having resolved an inner conflict between unbelief and faith. It means keeping options open long after we ought to have closed them. Jesus told his disciples that they were to be in the world but not of the world (John 17:6-16). They live in the world, but their hope lies beyond it. They do not conform to its standards and its unbelief. There will always be tension between the believer and the world. In part, doubt arises through having feet in the camps of both the world and the gospel—and being reluctant to make that break. For many people there is security in staying within something that is known (however unsatisfactory) just as there is unease about confronting the unknown. "Play safe!" is the motto of many. Some are reluctant to commit themselves to the gospel because it seems otherworldly. But the

New Testament sees commitment to the gospel as the essential starting point for developing a right attitude to the world. No longer need we be frightened by death; no longer are we hypnotized by wealth (Matthew 6:19-21). We are enabled to live in the world without giving in to its standards and its anxieties.

Doubt as a state of mind. Thomas found it difficult to believe that Jesus had risen from the dead. Jesus, knowing this, spoke these words to him: "Do not doubt but believe" (John 20:27). The Greek phrase used is quite difficult to translate into English. Greek has two forms of imperative. In other words, you can tell somebody to do something in two different ways. What is known as an aorist imperative means "do this action once." If I asked somebody to open a window, I would use this form. A second form, however, is the present imperative. This means "Keep on doing this! Don't just do it once!" The Greek verb used in John 20:27 is a present imperative. It doesn't mean "on this one occasion, don't doubt—believe instead!" Rather, it means "stop doubting now, once and for all. And keep on believing."

In other words, *doubt and faith are both states of mind or attitudes.* Doubt can be a constant attitude of questioning toward God, where faith can be a constant attitude of trust and openness. We are being asked to develop a permanent attitude of openness and trust toward God—not just to be open to him and trust him on any one occasion, but to be like this all the time. This results in conflict at times, since our old tendency to doubt God surfaces, but this just underscores our need to commit ourselves more fully to him again.

IMAGES OF THE NATURE AND EFFECTS OF DOUBT
Two images are particularly helpful in thinking about the nature

and effects of doubt—and in beginning to develop ways of handling it.

Walking in the dark. "Salvation is nearer to us now than when we became believers; the night is far gone, the day is near" (Romans 13:11-12). These phrases from Paul invite us to think of the Christian life as walking in the dark. The dawn is now nearer than when we first began that walk, but it has yet to happen. In the meantime, we have to cross an unknown landscape, hoping that we will arrive safely at our destination. We cannot fully see the road ahead of us; nevertheless, we trust in the Lord to guide us home. "For we walk by faith, not by sight" (2 Corinthians 5:7).

Imagine you are a traveler in medieval England. You decide to travel to the city of Oxford from the nearby village of Witney. Darkness falls as you near Oxford so that you cannot see the landscape around you. You decide to keep going along the road, despite the darkness. All you can see is the road ahead of you, which you know to have been signposted to Oxford. At times, there are things about that road which puzzle you. The road may turn abruptly to the left at one point. You wonder why. At another point, it becomes very muddy. Again, you wonder why. But you don't know. You can't see the full picture. You're in the dark.

Of course, when dawn breaks, you can see the landscape fully illuminated. Then the real state of things becomes apparent. You might suddenly notice that the road swerves to the left to avoid an open mineshaft, invisible to you in the dark. You might see that at one point the road passes close to a raging torrent, which might have swept you away, if the road had not led you away from it— as it turned out, all that happened was that your feet got a bit muddy. Although you could not understand what was happening at the time, you subsequently realize that the road led you in safety in the darkness through a series of dangers. Your initial bewilderment turns to relief.

The basic point here is that *we don't see the full picture.* God does; we don't. As Paul puts it, "we see in a mirror, dimly" (1 Corinthians 13:12). It's like being inside a car on a dark night, with the windows misted up. Or trying to make sense of a snapshot taken by a camera that wasn't properly in focus; it is blurred and fuzzy. The same problem arises: we can't see properly. And so often, we begin to doubt what lies beyond the window or the camera lens because the means of knowing things does not give us the clarity we believe we should expect. In the words of Blaise Pascal, "In faith there is enough light for those who want to believe and enough shadows to blind those who don't."

There are many things about the Christian life that puzzle us. Yet we have to learn to live with the fact that we will not, on earth, see the full picture, and for that very reason we will have to put up with areas of experience that seem contradictory and confused. Doubt can arise partly because we feel frustrated at not being able to understand everything. We want to stand in the place of God and be able to survey the landscape across which the path of faith must travel. Yet we can't. In fact, we can't really see further than the end of our spiritual noses!

We believe passionately and rightly that a road is there, that it will lead us safely to our goal, and that Jesus Christ has been along that road before us, like a pioneer or trailblazer (Hebrews 12:1-3). But we don't understand exactly what is going on at points. Our place is on that path, not above it. One day, we firmly believe, all will be made clear—but this will be on the far side of our resurrection! For the moment, however, we must walk through the darkness in faith and hope.

However, the landscape is not totally dark. The image of light is used frequently by scriptural writers, reminding us that God has not left us completely in the dark! Scripture itself guides us as we walk. "Your word is a lamp to my feet and a light to my path" (Psalm 119:105). This helpful image suggests illumination of an area around us while we walk, but not of the entire landscape. As Martin Luther King Jr. puts it, "Faith is taking the first step even when you don't see the whole staircase."

Again, it's like being in a car at night, with the headlights illuminating a small area just ahead of us. The important thing is that we find our way home, not that we understand exactly what is happening at every point along the way! The road really is there, tried and tested by previous generations of travelers.

The famous gospel image of a city on a hill (Matthew 5:14-16) makes the same point: a light shining in the darkness can guide us home. Take one step at a time, and don't be frightened by the thought of how long or difficult that journey might be. God will be with you, traveling alongside you and lighting your path as he accompanies you on your way.

So it is understandable that doubt should arise on account of our less than total grasp of the situation. We can't fully see the picture. But how could we, as finite creatures, ever hope to gain a total understanding of our situation? What really matters is the fact that God promises to be faithful to us, to remain with us as we travel, to guide us and support us, and that Christ has gone before us, to prepare a place for us. The gospel doesn't pretend to explain every aspect of our life as believers—it does, however, promise that God will be with us throughout life (Psalm 23). In the end it is the saving presence of God in the life of believers that matters more than a complete explanation of the way things are.

For Christians, we are walking a road that leads to the New Jerusalem. But we aren't on our own. Jesus has gone ahead of us, blazing the trail, and he accompanies us as we travel. Like a shepherd, he is with us throughout every moment of that journey. His loving care never changes or falters. Even when we travel through the valley of the shadow of death, he is there. We may not fully understand the details of that journey, but we know he is with us, by our sides, as we travel.

Rough sea. "The one who doubts is like a wave of the sea, driven and tossed by the wind" (James 1:6). This is a very powerful image (especially for anyone who has ever been violently seasick!), an image evoking a lack of stability. The sea—along with anything that happens to be floating in it—is tossed to and fro by the wind, unable to gain stability. Seasickness is basically caused by a disruption of the human sense of balance, arising from this instability. You lose your bearings, life is miserable, and you long for the ship to regain its stability. Doubt in the Christian life is rather like permanent seasickness on a long ocean voyage. So how can stability be regained?

God's faithfulness is like an anchor (Hebrews 6:18-19). He is true to his promises, giving us something that we can hold on to. Just as a ship being blown off course by a storm might lower its anchor, so faith in God gives us direction and stability in life. Faith is like a lifeline thrown to us in a raging sea: in the midst of this storm, the trustworthy promises of God offer us stability and safety. The death of Jesus Christ on the cross of Calvary demonstrates both God's overwhelming love for us, and his commitment to us. Nothing can cancel his faithfulness to us. Like a harbor, he offers refuge from the storms of life. Doubt means having nothing to hold on to in this situation; it can mean a lack of trust in the means of security God is offering us. Faith, on the other hand, means trusting the faithfulness of God and the reliability of the assistance he offers us (Psalm 119:35-40).

6

DOUBTS ABOUT THE GOSPEL

We live in a culture that values doubt and distrusts faith. No matter where we turn, we find criticism of commitment and commendation of questioning. Newspapers, magazines, university lectures, popular television programs and radio shows reinforce the values of our postmodern culture. Commitment is a bad thing! Look at Stalinism. Or Nazism. That's what commitment does to people. It turns them into intolerant fundamentalists. The sound bites accumulate, reinforcing Western culture's core beliefs at the moment: all beliefs are equally valid. The important thing is to be sincere and kind, and not hurt anyone.

Christians cannot isolate themselves from these pressures. They experience them when they read magazines, listen to the radio, go to lectures on campus or visit the shopping mall. The important point to appreciate is that sometimes our doubts about the gospel arise from cultural pressures, not from the gospel itself. Our postmodern culture encourages doubt and detests commitment. So let's look at this culture in a little more detail. It's a complicated melting pot of ideas and attitudes.

Many are *cynical*. We believe things, they argue, simply because it suits us. These people are often highly critical of any kind of religious belief. They say that religious belief is just a crutch for sad and inadequate people, who want to run away from the harsh reality of life—a life that has no meaning, no purpose and no goal. "Life is just a dirty trick from nothingness to nothingness" (Ernest Hemingway). Let's grow up, they tell us, and get rid of such childish ideas.

Others are *relativists,* suspicious of anyone who claims to know things with any confidence. Only fools, they tell us, would believe something so naive. All viewpoints are equally good—or, from another perspective, equally bad. The only thing we can be certain about is that there are no certainties. We just need to be openminded and tolerant. As the social commentator Alan Bloom once remarked, we seem to live in a culture that regards commitment as the ultimate sin.

Now these views are very influential, but that doesn't mean they are right. The wisdom of our age is often seen as an embarrassment by the next generation. When I was an atheist, back in the late 1960s, everything seemed so simple. Religion was dying out. A bright new dawn lay just around the corner. Religion would be relegated to the past, a grim and dusty relic of a bygone age. God was just a cozy illusion for losers, ideal for very inadequate and sad people. It was all over, just a matter of waiting for nature to take its course. I was in good company in believing this sort of thing. It was the smug, foolish and fashionable wisdom of the age. Like bellbottom jeans, it was accepted enthusiastically, if just a little uncritically. But it just hasn't worked out like that. These ideas may have been fashionable. They were certainly influential. But they were equally certainly misguided.

Let's look at one of these cultural pressures briefly, before moving on. One of the most widely encountered slogans on university campuses or radio shows goes like this: *you can't be certain of anything*. Really? The people who believe this sort of thing often fail to appreciate the contradiction. You can't be certain of anything—except this statement that I have just made, which is the exception to this universal rule. The truth is much more complicated, as you might expect, and it has to do with showing that there are adequate grounds for what we believe. And for Christians, that is not a problem, as we will see.

The important thing here is to realize that our culture has certain inbuilt assumptions, which it assumes to be self-evidently correct. But on closer inspection, they turn out to be nothing of the sort. The problems that our culture has with the Christian faith are not a reflection on the faith itself. The problems lie within the culture.

The veneration of doubt and the excoriation of commitment within our culture do not mean that the gospel is *wrong*. It just means that our culture is going through a passing phase that brings it into conflict with the values of that gospel. And the culture will move on, even though it makes life uncomfortable for us now!

Yet every culture—whether modern or postmodern—creates both obstacles and opportunities for faith. Thus far, I have highlighted the problems, as these are likely to be experienced by Christians working within postmodern culture. But I must stress that there are also opportunities. Postmodernity may cause us difficulties at some points, closing doors that once were open—but it also opens new doors. Let me explain what I mean.

The rise of postmodernity reflects disillusionment with the worldview that we usually call modernity. This latter movement, which swept through Western culture in the eighteenth century and had such a major impact on the nineteenth and twentieth centuries, is now in decline. The hopes that modernity had brought—such as the expected triumph of reason and science, which many thought would usher in a new age of peace, prosperity and progress—have failed in just about every respect. As many sociologists have pointed out, atheism is the natural religion of modernity. But with the rise of postmodernity, everything has changed. There is a new hunger for spiritual matters, reflected in a deep-seated awareness that modernity has failed to answer humanity's deepest questions.

Christianity has much to say here, connecting with the most profound longings of humanity. As writers such as Pascal and C. S. Lewis have argued, these longings are ultimately a secret desire for God, which nothing else can satisfy. We may live in a *doubting* culture—but it is also a *longing* culture that knows it is searching for something that it has not yet found. There is so much that Christianity has to say here!

With this point in mind, let us move on to consider two anxieties about the gospel itself. Some young Christians, especially students, often have a secret uneasiness about the future of Christianity. Will it go out of date? Are they committing themselves to something that may become irrelevant in their old age? A second anxiety concerns the effectiveness of the gospel. Some Christians become despondent on account of the apparent ineffectiveness of their attempts to proclaim the gospel, and they sometimes wonder if this reflects some fundamental weakness, perhaps even a fatal flaw, in the gospel itself. I will address these anxieties in what follows.

WILL CHRISTIANITY GO OUT OF FASHION SOMETIME?

We live in times when everything seems to become obsolete very quickly. The latest technology makes old methods and equipment go out of date with alarming speed. And it isn't just hardware that gets outdated in this way. Ideas go out of fashion very quickly. I grew up in the 1960s, when it seemed to many that the Western world was going through a period of revolution. The old ideas and standards were being thrown out as irrelevant. We were told that the world had come of age and that it no longer needed the outdated ideas of past generations. There was much talk of the "death of God" on the university campuses of North America and elsewhere. Christianity was portrayed as outmoded and irrelevant to the needs of this brave new world.

Of course, the 1960s were a long time ago. Looking back, I realize that it is the ideas of the 1960s that have become outdated. They've gone out of fashion. Instead of being a permanent feature of the way we think, they were shown up to be a response to the needs of that period. As time passed and the situation changed, they lost their credibility. They had a shelf life of a decade or so before they became unmarketable. Christianity has been a powerful force in the world for nearly two thousand years and shows no sign of losing its appeal. Marxism argued that, when the revolution came, Christianity would be abandoned as outdated and pointless; in fact, the reverse occurred, a new interest in the Christian faith developed within Marxist states, despite government programs designed to eliminate it. And then Marxism itself collapsed in the 1990s. In America in the 1960s, it was suggested that there was an urgent need to find an alternative religion, on account of the new outlook on life that was allegedly developing in Western civilization. But, as history has shown, it was that new outlook on life, rather than Christianity, which was found to be irrelevant to the needs and aspirations of human beings.

But this does raise an important question. Is Christianity itself something that will go out of fashion in the future? As time passes, and the human situation changes, will the gospel cease to be relevant? After all, nobody believes in the old Roman or Greek gods anymore—yet they seem to have been influential for a while. This is a cause of special concern to college and university students: is the Christian gospel in which they have placed their trust (or in which they are thinking of placing their trust) something to which they can hold fast to for the remainder of their lives? Or will it cease to have any relevance after a decade? Doubts of this kind trouble a number of young Christians and may cause others to hesitate before committing themselves. Therefore, it is important to deal with this question fully.

Two answers may be given to this doubt. First, the gospel addresses a fundamental problem of human nature, which progress hasn't altered. Second, if it really is God who is behind the gospel, it cannot lose its power and appeal. We'll look at these individually.

The human dilemma remains the same. The gospel is not some form of human wisdom that will be outdated within a matter of years, but it is an eternally relevant message concerning God and ourselves—and supremely the relationship established through the death and resurrection of Jesus Christ. The human dilemma remains the same yesterday, today and forever: the need to be loved, the need to have hope in the face of death, the need to break free from sin. The gospel identifies these deep longings and needs within human nature.

The gospel does not, however, merely diagnose the human situation; it offers to transform it. It doesn't just identify our problems, but proclaims their solution. It affirms the overwhelming

love of God for us as sinners and draws our attention to the astonishing extent to which God will go to demonstrate that love. It offers to break the stranglehold of human sin, setting us free to live
with God. It offers us a firm and unshakable hope in the face of
death. And so long as human beings walk the face of this earth,
knowing that they must die, the gospel of the resurrection of Jesus
Christ will continue to address a basic human need. Let's develop
this point a little.

In his classic work *The Denial of Death,* Ernest Becker pointed
out how much human activity is based on illusion (or denial). Un-
like other animals, humans know that they are going to die and
cannot cope with the thought. They spend much of their time trying to deny the inevitability of death, creating the illusion that
death is always something that happens to somebody else. Death
is something people prefer not to talk about because of the anxiety
it causes, so life comes to be a desperate denial of human mortality.
This denial is merely a crutch on which many are totally dependent for their sanity. Death, as someone once grimly remarked, is
the ultimate statistic.

But how can anyone base their entire life on a total delusion?
Running away from reality won't change the situation. It is perfectly
understandable that people should be afraid of death. But that is
precisely why the gospel is so important and so relevant! Through
his death and resurrection, Jesus Christ is able to "free those who all
their lives were held in slavery by the fear of death" (Hebrews 2:15).
This power to liberate individuals from the fear of death is not some
afterthought, but is central to the gospel theme. The gospel does not
evade human mortality, nor run away from its challenge. Rather, it
joyfully and confidently proclaims that Jesus Christ died and rose
again so that we might have eternal life.

The gospel is the work of God, not a human invention. When Paul preached the gospel at Corinth, he was acutely aware of his own deficiencies as a preacher. Yet the gospel took root there, despite this. He wrote thus to the church at Corinth later concerning his poor performance (1 Corinthians 2:1-5):

> When I came to you, brothers and sisters, I did not come proclaiming the mystery of God to you in lofty words or wisdom. For I decided to know nothing among you except Jesus Christ, and him crucified. And I came to you in weakness and in fear and in much trembling. My speech and my proclamation were not with plausible words of wisdom, but with a demonstration of the Spirit and of power, so that your faith might rest not on human wisdom but on the power of God.

Can you see what Paul is saying here? The gospel that he proclaimed, and which won the hearts and minds of the Corinthian Christians, is not a human invention but is the work of God.

Much the same point is made elsewhere in the New Testament. "We did not follow cleverly devised myths when we made known to you the power and coming of our Lord Jesus, but we had been eyewitnesses of his majesty" (2 Peter 1:16). In other words, the gospel isn't based on human wisdom or invention, but on the revelation of God in history, seen and attested by eyewitnesses. The death and resurrection of Jesus were no fiction or legend—they were events in history, seen and proclaimed by the first Christians (1 Corinthians 15:3-8).

If you accept the gospel, you may rest assured that you are not committing intellectual suicide by falling victim to some fleeting whim that will have passed into the footnotes of history books within a few years. The gospel has been around for over two thousand years; it is not like some cult, craze or fashion, which is abandoned when something else takes its place. And why not? Because we are not dealing with some human invention, some ideas that somebody thought up, but we are dealing with the gracious self-revelation of God himself, a revelation that both declares and meets the spiritual needs of humanity. Whoever you are and wherever you live, the gospel has the power to convert you, and having converted you to hold you, which human wisdom alone cannot do. It is God's gospel, the gospel he revealed in his Son, Jesus, and through Jesus' death on the cross of Calvary and his resurrection.

If God really is behind the gospel, it cannot fail in the end. In his wisdom and his love, God has given to us the good news of forgiveness through the death and resurrection of Jesus Christ. Your faith rests not in human wisdom (which is likely to be rejected by later generations), but in the power of God—the same God who was able to raise Jesus Christ from the dead, transforming a scene of hopelessness and helplessness to one of joy and triumph. This is the kind of God who inspires confidence. Your friends may think you foolish for your faith, as others thought Paul foolish before you—but you may rest assured, as Paul did, that the gospel which has touched your heart today is not from human beings but from God, and it will continue to proclaim the saving love of God in Christ until he comes again.

THE GOSPEL SEEMS TO HAVE LITTLE EFFECT ON MY FRIENDS

It's a big decision, committing yourself to God. Let's put this in perspective. You ask your friends to dedicate their lives to someone, to Jesus Christ. Now that's a lot to ask, by any standards! So you must expect a certain degree of hesitation on their part. They will want to weigh the consequences. They will want to think the matter through. They won't want to rush into it. That's reasonable.

In fact, it's such a big decision that many people prefer to take it in small stages. Think of each individual having a personal road to faith. Everyone has different needs and problems, with the result that it's difficult to lay down in advance what a "typical" conversion might be like. For some, that road may be relatively short and easy. But for others, it may be long and difficult. Think of yourself as helping them a little further along that road or helping them around obstacles strewn in their path. You may not help them all the way to the final destination, but you can leave them nearer to it than when they started. They may end up feeling much more positive toward Christianity and toward Christians on account of you. Perhaps they may find they have fewer difficulties with some of its ideas as a result of talking to you. Maybe you've planted some seeds that will germinate later. Now it's quite likely that they won't admit this, so you may not realize what's happening. And so you may get discouraged.

Jesus told a parable that is helpful and relevant here. Mark 4:26-29 relates how someone scatters seed on the ground and then leaves it. The seed grows in secret, eventually to break through the ground and mature. Most commentators on this passage see it as referring to the hidden work of the kingdom of God in the world. Its effects are not initially seen; it is growing in secret, like the seed beneath the ground. Though it can't be seen, that doesn't mean it's not there. The parable makes clear the importance of sowing the seed (see also Ecclesiastes 11:6). That's our responsibility. But it is God who makes the seed grow (see 1 Corinthians 3:6-7), even if that process of growth can't be seen until the seedling bursts through the soil.

One of my favorite books is *The Diary of a Nobody*. It's a fictional diary recording the problems and aspirations of a lower middle-class man (Mr. Pooter) and his family in late Victorian London. At one point the diary tells of how Mr. Pooter sowed some seeds in his garden one evening. The entries for the next few days all record his growing desperation. Each day he inspects his seeds—and nothing has happened! There is something of Mr. Pooter in all of us: we want to see instant results from our witness to our friends. We think conversion is something that must happen in the short term. But for many, conversion is a prolonged experience. Your contribution may be to move them further down the road to faith, but not to bring them to its goal.

Have you noticed how often Jesus returns to the theme of the goodness of the seed? The parable of the sower (Mark 4:3-8) stresses that it is the same good seed that falls into different kinds of ground. There's nothing wrong with the seed—it's the ground that makes the difference. What is important is that you scatter the seed—you cannot be sure what sort of ground it will fall on. Some seed may be sown to no effect (perhaps being eaten by birds)—but that does not mean that the next seed you sow will fail to grow! Again, the seed may not seem to be growing (Mark 4:26-29)—but, as Mr. Pooter eventually found out, that doesn't mean that there's anything wrong with it. It's important to have confidence in the power of the gospel and trust that God will do his good work with the seed that takes root through our witness. If the seed was no good, Christianity would have ceased to exist long ago.

It's helpful to think of Paul here. Try and imagine how the early church felt about Saul of Tarsus. Saul was, by all accounts, one of the most efficient persecutors of Christianity (Acts 8:1; 9:1-2). In a later letter, he recalled how intensely he persecuted the church and how he tried to wipe it off the face of the earth (Galatians 1:13). Those first Christians could have been forgiven for thinking that Saul was an impossible case. Here, surely, was a nut that was too hard to crack. The gospel was having no visible effect on him. They must have been very discouraged.

The remarkable story of Paul's conversion through his encounter with the risen Christ (Acts 9:1-19; 22:2-16; 26:12-23) reminds us of two things. First, it is God who is at work in the process of conversion. It isn't as if someone is converted on account of our eloquence, wisdom or arguments. In the end, conversion is about a transforming and redeeming encounter between an individual and the living Lord. We can help bring that about—but that encounter is God's doing, not ours. Second, it reminds us that the most unpromising outward appearances may conceal hidden signs of the work of God. Don't be anxious—trust instead in the gospel and the God who stands behind it.

In dealing with these two anxieties, you may find it helpful to read the story of the upper room (John 20:19-31). From that room a very small group of people went out to convert the world—a seemingly impossible mission. Yet your faith can be traced back to that upper room. You have a spiritual family tree, which connects you with someone who was there in that upper room on that momentous occasion. Through the faithfulness of that person, and those who followed him or her, you came to faith. That remarkable fact points to the power of the gospel to reach down through the ages, across both centuries and continents. That ought to reassure you of its relevance and vitality! But it ought also to challenge you to ask a very important question. The great chain of events that leads from the upper room to you—where will it go next? To whom will you pass on the gospel proclamation?

7

DOUBTS ABOUT YOURSELF

A second group of anxieties centers on our own relationship with God, and especially on our adequacy as Christians. Some Christians find it difficult to have any confidence in themselves. As a result, they find it hard to enter into Christian life in all its fullness, with both its privileges and responsibilities. Unease over whether you really are a Christian, uncertainty over your abilities or anxiety concerning your inadequacies—all these can induce a kind of mental and spiritual paralysis, preventing you from developing and growing in faith and obedience. I hope that this chapter will alleviate some of these anxieties.

I'M NOT SURE THAT I AM A CHRISTIAN

This doubt is often experienced by people who have become Christians recently. How, they may ask, can they know that they are Christians? Is there something they can point to that proves they really have been accepted by God? Is there some visible sign that proves they have entered into the kingdom of God? The early stage of faith is often a very vulnerable period, and it is not uncommon for Christians in their first stage of development to feel anxious about their relationship with God.

But it is important not to always rely on our feelings. In the following section, I will explore how feelings can sometimes be unreliable as a guide to our standing with God. Feelings are tied up with many things, as well as with our relationship with God. We may feel far from God because of anxiety over our career, our work, a personal relationship or financial difficulties. All of these can easily spill over into our perception of our relationship with God.

Instead, we should rely on the promises of God. These are outside of us, independent of our feelings and anxieties. Feelings are subjective; God's promises are objective. They don't depend on feelings. For example, look at God's promise to Joshua (Joshua 1:9). God promises to be with Joshua wherever he goes. He doesn't promise to be with Joshua on the condition that Joshua *feels* that God is present! The promise of the presence of God is unconditional. We must learn to mistrust our feelings at this point. "Be still and know that I am God" (Psalm 46:10). We ought to ground our faith in the promises of God recorded in Scripture, and confirmed in Jesus Christ—not the way we feel.

What sort of promises might these be? In one sense these promises *are* conditional: they depend on us having repented of our sins and turned to God in faith. Faith is saying "yes" to God, and learning to trust in him, to know him better and to be obedient to him. The Greek word usually translated as *repent* has the basic meaning of "turn around." We must turn around to face God (how many people spend their lives running away from God?), admitting our sins and accepting God's offer of forgiveness and eternal life. That can be painful and difficult, for it involves admitting our need for God. Think of God offering you a gift. To receive it, you must stretch out your hand and take it. The offer is real, as is the gift;

your acceptance of the offer must be real as well. And if you have accepted that offer, then you are a Christian. The promises of God are yours.

God loves sinners. First, there is the promise that God, while detesting sin, loves sinners. "God proves his love for us in that while we still were sinners Christ died for us" (Romans 5:8). The full extent of this love is revealed in the cross of Christ. Jesus died in order to convince and assure us of the tender love of God for us sinners (John 3:16), and thus to bring us home to God. Some people think that they are too deeply immersed in their sin to be loved by God; the New Testament happens to take a very different view, affirming that nothing can separate us from the love of God in Christ (Romans 8:31-39). God's purpose and power to defeat sin are revealed in the cross. To suggest or imagine that your sin is somehow worse than anyone else's is to deny God the opportunity to break its power in your life. Try to imagine the situation Paul found himself in. How could God love him, when he had persecuted the church of God? If anyone ever felt convinced of sin and personal inadequacy, that person was Paul. Yet Paul was able to draw on the tender mercy of God toward sinners and to speak of the remarkable effects of God's grace in his life (1 Corinthians 15:9-10).

There is a story about the Scottish pastor and writer John Duncan that is relevant here. Duncan was conducting a Communion service in a local Church of Scotland parish. When he came to administer the wine to the congregation, a sixteen-year-old girl refused to accept it. She motioned with her hand, indicating that she did not feel able to share in the cup. Realizing that the girl felt unworthy to receive it, Duncan reached out, laid his arm on her shoulder, and said: "Take it lassie. It's meant for us sinners." The wine is a symbol of God's forgiveness of sins through the death of Christ—real forgiveness of real sins. To recognize the full extent of our sinfulness is not to disqualify ourselves from the grace of God—it is to indicate how much we need it.

God forgives sins. Second, we are promised forgiveness of sins (1 John 1:9). To become a Christian is to set the past behind us, to go forward into eternal life in the presence of the God who loved us and gave his only son for us. Through the cross, the burden of our sin is taken from us by Christ, and his righteousness becomes ours (2 Corinthians 5:21). This promise of forgiveness, however, does not merely concern the beginning of our lives as Christians. We don't stop sinning when we become Christians! Rather, we begin a long and hard struggle against sin. It can be very difficult at times. We may often feel that we have let God down. But we must learn to trust in God's immense kindness and tenderness: ask his forgiveness of these sins and start out all over again. Being a Christian isn't easy, as the New Testament stresses. All of us find it difficult going at times, which is why the news that God forgives us for our shortcomings and weaknesses is such good news.

God will never leave or forsake us. Third, we are promised that God will stand by us in our lives as Christians (John 10:28). He is with us always (Matthew 28:20). No matter how we may feel, God has promised to remain with us. He is the shepherd who guides us and guards us, who journeys with us, consoling us with his presence (Psalm 23). There is no small print here, qualifying this promise! God promises himself to all those who turn to him in faith.

Have you turned to God in faith and repentance? If you have, these promises concern you. You may feel that your faith is very weak. But, as I have stressed, faith is like a plant—it is something that grows. The weakness and fragility of its early stages give way to the strength and maturity of its later phases. Some seeds germinate more rapidly than others, just as some plants grow more quickly than others. Be patient! Remember that a house built quickly is usually a house built badly—it won't survive. After all, Rome wasn't built in a day. This slow and gradual growth in faith reflects human weakness and fragility, not any inability on God's part. God knows what we are like and how best to handle us. As Paul stresses (1 Corinthians 3:10-13), the Christian life is built securely on a reliable foundation. If the seed of faith is firmly planted, it will grow—despite its initial fragility and vulnerability. The important thing is not that your faith is strong, but that you have faith! Like Paul, you can be "confident of this, that he who began a good work in you will carry it on to completion" (Philippians 1:6; cf. 2 Peter 1:3-4).

You may worry that your faith is weak. Yet your salvation does not depend on the strength of your faith, but on the power of the one in whom you believe. The great Scottish preacher and hymnwriter of the nineteenth century Horatio Bonar knew doubt firsthand and wrote some words in *The Everlasting Righteousness* that may be helpful here:

> With a weak faith and a fearful heart, many a sinner stands before the Lord. It is not the strength of our faith, but the perfection of Christ's sacrifice that saves! No feebleness of faith, nor dimness of eye, no trembling of hand can change the efficacy of Christ's blood. The strength of our faith can add nothing to it, nor can the weakness of our faith take anything from Him. Faith (weak or strong) still reads the promise, "the blood of Jesus Christ His Son cleanses us from all

sin." If at times my eye is so dim that I cannot read these words, through blinding tears or bewildering trials, faith rests itself on the certain knowledge of the fact that THE PROMISE IS THERE, and the blood of Christ remains in all its power and suitableness upon the altar, unchanged and unaffected.

Be assured that God has done everything necessary for your salvation, and has done it well. Your salvation does not depend on your personal merit, or your activity, or even the strength of your faith. God offers you his salvation—real salvation—as a gift. You are being asked to receive it, to accept it and make it your own. Julian of Norwich, a medieval English nun, wrote a fascinating book titled *Revelations of Divine Love,* in which she stated, "The one thing that matters is that we always say Yes to God when we experience him." Say "yes!"—and all that God is and all that he means can be yours. Two illustrations may prove helpful.

Imagine that you are in a darkened room. Outside, the sunlight is beaming down. However, there is a shutter in front of the window, preventing the light from entering. You can open that shutter. By doing so, you are removing the only remaining obstacle to the light of the sun, allowing it to illuminate the room. You are not being asked to undertake the mammoth task of generating the heat and light of the sun—that has all been taken care of for you. Your sole task—but a task that only you can do—is to remove an obstacle to its passage. It is a relatively small task, but an essential one. If you have anxieties about whether you really are a Christian, ask yourself whether there are any remaining obstacles to God. Are you holding back from him? Ask God to illuminate your life with his light, and throw open wide the shutters of your heart. Ask him to come in, and make him welcome as your guest and master.

Or imagine a giant hydroelectric system, like the Hoover Dam. Think of the enormous power of countless millions of gallons of water, cascading down to drive the great generators that give power to nearby cities. That power is available, at the throw of a switch. It can be yours. You don't have to generate it yourself: that has been done for you. It is something on which you can rely. But you must make connection with it. Think of your repentance and acceptance of God's forgiveness as being like throwing a switch, which allows forgiveness and power to surge into your life. Have you thrown that switch? If so, all else has been done for you, and you can rest assured that God is working within your life, slowly but surely. To be a Christian is to trust in the promises of God and be obedient to him. You may not feel that God is present—but your feelings are not necessarily reliable.

I DON'T EXPERIENCE GOD AS BEING PRESENT IN MY LIFE

Many Christians, especially those who have experienced a dramatic conversion experience, begin with a very strong sense of God's closeness. God seems very near and very real. The whole world seems to vibrate with his presence. There is a sense in which all of creation seems to tingle with the glory of God. After a while, however, this experience of the presence of God begins to wane. For some Christians, God is no longer experienced as present. Doubt begins to settle in. Perhaps you feel anxious about the validity of that initial experience. Was it all just an emotional release, without any real substance?

There are many things that need to be said in response to such an anxiety. To begin with, let's look at a great biblical event that il-

lustrates very well the point involved. Think about the exodus
from Egypt, when Israel broke free from its Egyptian bondage,
crossed the Red Sea and began its long pilgrimage to the Promised
Land. In the early days of the exodus, God was obviously active
and present. The pillars of cloud and fire were visible symbols and
reminders of the presence and power of the Lord among his people (Exodus 13:20-21). The crossing of the Red Sea (Exodus 14)
confirmed this. But soon, discontent set in. Those who had been
set free from bondage began to doubt the Lord and demanded that
he be put to the test. Was he really there? Was the long journey
worth all the effort? Did God know what he was doing? As the
march through the desert wilderness continued year after year,
doubts grew stronger. God was not experienced as present.

Of course, God was indeed present during that period of wandering in the wilderness. With the triumphant entry into the
Promised Land, the people's confidence in the Lord was fully restored, and their doubts in the wilderness were revealed for what
they were. But think of yourself in their situation in the wilderness. To start with, God seemed very close. You could hardly ignore his presence. But as the years wore on, the memory of that
early period seemed unreliable. Perhaps you had just imagined it.
God didn't seem to be experienced as present any more.

You can understand how they felt—but how unreliable those
feelings turned out to be! God had promised to be present with his
people wherever they went. That promise was grounded in the
faithfulness of God, not in their subjective impressions of whether
God was there or not.

In your early days as a Christian, you may have known a spiritual equivalent of those pillars of cloud and fire—an experience, a
feeling, of the presence and power of God. There may have been

something like the parting of the Red Sea, when God confirmed that he was really present and active in your life—perhaps an answered prayer, perhaps some kind of sign. Maybe that was some time ago. Now you may feel doubtful about your early feelings. But can you see how unreliable feelings are in deciding whether God is there or not? Or whether he cares for you or not? Or whether he knows what he is doing? Christianity is firmly grounded in the faithfulness of God to his promises, not our feelings. Like Israel, you may find that something will happen to restore your experience of the presence of God.

Experience depends as much on your mental state as on the way things really are. It is perfectly possible for these two statements to be true at one and the same time:

1. God is there.

2. I don't experience God as being there.

No contradiction is involved. One of the most moving descriptions of the feeling that God is not there is found in Psalm 42. The psalmist here speaks as someone in the depths of spiritual despair. He is downcast, dispirited and anxious. He feels far from God. His friends have noticed this and make fun of him. "Where's this God of yours, then?" Yet despite this, he knows that God is still there. He remembers the good times, the times when he was close to God and knew it, and he takes enormous comfort from the knowledge—grounded in his confidence in the absolute faithfulness and trustworthiness of God—that this time of depression and despair will pass. The psalm thus ends with a note of faith, even of triumph: "Hope in God; for I shall again praise him, / my help and my God."

Notice what the psalmist does *not* do. He doesn't pretend that his feelings of doubt and anxiety do not exist. Instead, he acknowledges them and brings them before the Lord. He knows that, despite his feelings, God is still there, just as a cloud may pass in front of the sun and temporarily cut off its light. The cloud will pass, and the sun will once more come into view. As Charles Haddon Spurgeon puts it in *Faith's Checkbook*, "It is not hard for the Lord to turn night into day. He that sends the clouds can as easily clear the skies. Let us be of good cheer. It is better farther on. Let us sing Hallelujah by anticipation."

Remember that it isn't just you who have experienced this sense of the absence of God all on your own. This isn't something new. It isn't something that has never happened before. And it doesn't mean that you're a lousy Christian. For example, it's a frequent theme in the writings of Martin Luther (the great German reformer) and John of the Cross (a Spanish spiritual writer of the sixteenth century). You can turn to writers like these, who draw on their own experience and the experience of the people who they've counseled, as they affirm God's total faithfulness to his promises, despite the temporary feeling of his absence. Take some comfort from the thought that many other Christians have had these feelings before you and have gone on to tell of how they resolved them.

An excellent example of this is provided by Psalm 13. The psalm opens with the psalmist expressing his deep and despondent sense of the absence of God. "How long, O LORD? Will you forget me forever? / How long will you hide your face from me? / How long must I bear pain in my soul, / and have sorrow in my heart all day long?" (verses 1-2). Perhaps you can identify with his position, sympathizing with his sadness at the feeling of God's absence. Perhaps you are experiencing such feelings even now. However, instead of becoming increasingly introverted, contemplating his own state of anxiety, the psalmist turns to contemplate the character of God: his trustworthiness, his covenant faithfulness and his loving kindness. The psalm thus ends with a sense of hope and expectation. "But I trusted in your steadfast love; / my heart shall rejoice in your salvation. / I will sing to the LORD, / because he has dealt bountifully with me" (verses 5-6).

Note how the psalmist turns to praise at this point. Praise can help throw off the sense of gloom that sometimes comes with doubt. Note also the decisive turn away from feelings toward the promises and character of God himself. It's very easy to get trapped in a rut of depression, to keep looking inward, examining feelings and emotions, and allowing these to determine our spiritual state. Instead, we should turn outward, away from our feelings, and contemplate instead the promises of a trustworthy and faithful God, which culminated in the death and resurrection of Jesus Christ. "For in him every one of God's promises is a 'Yes' " (2 Corinthians 1:20). Turn outward to other people, who can set your anxieties in perspective.

Finally, remember the advice that C. S. Lewis's Screwtape gave his nephew Wormwood in the sixth Screwtape Letter. The best way to make Christians into atheists is to stop them thinking about God and get them thinking about their own states of mind about God! Get them hopelessly preoccupied with their feelings and doubts, and stop them turning to God. Make them wallow in their uncertainties, so that they get despondent and discouraged. As C. S. Lewis knew, the certainty and security of the presence of God can easily be displaced by near-total doubt, simply by fixing our attention on our mental state, rather than on God himself.

I FEEL SO INADEQUATE AS A CHRISTIAN

When you consider the enormous responsibility and challenge of being a Christian, it's hardly surprising if you feel overwhelmed by it all. On the one hand there is the task of proclaiming the gospel to the world for which Christ died. On the other there is the task of ensuring that the love of God is expressed in lifestyles and programs of social and political action. The love of God draws us out of the world, only to send us back into it, as we try to transform the world in the light of the vision provided by the gospel.

Perhaps we feel rather like Joshua as he stood poised on the frontiers of the Promised Land and contemplated the awesome responsibility that had just been placed on his shoulders. Moses, the great man who had led Israel out of Egypt and through the wilderness, was dead; he, Joshua, had been chosen by God and entrusted with the task of leading his people into the Promised Land (Joshua 1:1-5). Joshua must have felt very inadequate in the face of such a challenge. But being given responsibilities by God carries with it the promise of being given assistance by God. It isn't as if God tells us to do something incredibly difficult and leaves us to get on with it on our own. God's gifts are tailored to God's demands. He knows our weaknesses and our abilities, and he matches his demands to those abilities. God's words to Joshua contain both command and promise—the command to lead his people into the Promised Land, and the promise that he, the living God, will be present with Joshua, sustaining and supporting him wherever he goes. "I hereby command you: Be strong and courageous; do not be frightened or dismayed, for the LORD your God will be with you wherever you go" (Joshua 1:9).

Or think of the apostles in those hectic days after the resurrection of Jesus. Only eleven in number, they were solemnly charged with the task of making disciples of all nations (Matthew 28:18-20). Imagine eleven people being told that they had to go and convert the whole world! You could understand if they felt a sense of despair, disbelief and total inadequacy. "Eleven of us against the world? You must be kidding!" Yet the reality of the situation was actually rather different: it was eleven of them and the living God against the world. Jesus told the apostles not to attempt anything until they had received "the gift my Father promised" (Acts 1:4 NIV; see also John 16:33). Their task required special divine assistance—which was duly provided at the first Pentecost, when God poured out his life-giving and enabling Spirit on the apostles (Acts 2:1-12). Once more, God matched the needs of the situation to his gifts.

The basic pattern that emerges here is that of God enabling ordinary and inadequate people to allow them to achieve their calling. The same pattern is repeated in the lives of Christians down through the centuries, as it can be in yours as well. Try reading the stories of some of the great missionaries and evangelists. Try reading the biographies of some famous Christians, and see how God works in their lives. God bestows gifts to enable them to meet their challenges and opportunities in his service. As we survey the enormous tasks that confront the modern church and try to establish what contribution we can make, it is important to realize that we are not working unaided. We are, to use Paul's wonderful phrase, "coworkers with God." Yet we are not equal partners, sharing the load evenly: it is God who plays the major part. Do your best—trust in God to do the rest. "The one who calls you is faithful, and he will do this" (1 Thessalonians 5:24).

God uses you—but, in the end, he doesn't depend on you. The

graveyards of the world are full of people who imagined that the success of the gospel depended on them—yet the grave could not hold the one on whom that success really depends. It is not us but the risen Christ who sustains the gospel that we proclaim. See yourself as a channel through which the power and activity of the risen Christ can be directed into the world. It's not what you are that matters—it's what you let God do with you and through you!

Some Christians are crippled or depressed by a feeling of uselessness. They feel that they are worthless. God's love affirms our personal worth yet does not depend on our worthiness or merit. As Martin Luther wrote, "Sinners are attractive because they are loved; they are not loved because they are attractive." Think of the overwhelming love of God shown for us in the death of Christ on the cross. See God affirming our personal worth. We are so important to God that Christ died for us. We matter to God—that is why he has chosen and called us.

Some Christians, however, suffer from a sense of spiritual pride, which leads them to trust more and more in their own abilities and rely less and less on the Lord. In this case, an awareness or recognition of their personal inadequacy can be an excellent asset. If we know that we are inadequate, we are less likely to have delusions about being able to manage by ourselves, and so we can learn to turn to the Lord in prayer and expectation. We look to him for inspiration, guidance and empowering. Being a Christian is a bit like being an electric motor: we need an external source of power. If we get disconnected from it, we're not much use.

Jesus used a more powerful analogy to make the same point: Christians are like branches on a vine (John 15:1-8). If the branch gets cut off from the vine, it withers away. It can only survive, and will only bear fruit, if it remains firmly attached to the vine and is able to draw on its life-giving sap. The branch is not independent, but relies totally on the vine for its life and its purpose—to yield fruit. Apart from Christ we can do nothing—and a sense of our own inadequacy prevents us from getting the idea that we can do anything much without turning to him. We must be receptive toward God, awaiting the gifts that he will give us to equip us for the tasks ahead.

Humility. Humility, then, is a very important virtue for a Christian. But humility is very easily misunderstood. If there is one thing that humility isn't, it is pretending that we have no special gifts or talents. (You might find it helpful to pray through Romans 12:3-8 or 1 Corinthians 12:4-11 alone or with a friend, asking for guidance on what gifts you possess.) Some Christians think that to be humble they need to deny that they have any talents. This isn't humility—it's false modesty! Humility is about recognizing that our gifts and talents, whatever and however many they may be, are gifts of God, which owe nothing to our personal worthiness and owe everything to his generosity and loving kindness. "What do you have that you did not receive?" (1 Corinthians 4:7).

The parable of the talents (Matthew 25:14-30) makes this point especially well. It tells of a master who entrusts his money to some servants during his absence—and of the variety of ways the servants make use of that money. There are three main points being made by this parable.

Our talents are gifts from God. The servants had no claim on the money: it was their master's, entrusted to them during his absence. In one sense, it was a gift to them—but a gift they would eventually have to surrender. They were stewards, rather than possessors, of the money. They were responsible for its wise use during the master's absence. In much the same way, we have been entrusted with gifts from God—not due to our personal worthiness but because of the tasks and responsibilities that God may have in mind for us.

No one is totally devoid of talents, however modest they may be about them. The important thing is to identify what your particular gifts might be as the first step in using them in God's service. Many people pray to know the will of God in their lives without realizing that his gifts to us can express his will for us! If your gifts happen to meet real needs somewhere in the world, it's quite possible that's where God wants you to be. Identifying the gifts God has given you is a useful way of beginning to discern God's will for your life.

How can you do that? Some talents are obvious—for example, you might be a very efficient organizer, a patient listener or an accomplished musician. You may be aware of such talents in yourself and challenged to think through how they could be used to further the kingdom of God. Very often, however, personal gifts and talents are best discerned by others. It might be worth your while talking this through with some close friends who can speak frankly about you.

In addition to discovering what you are good at, you may also discover what you aren't good at! Don't be ashamed if your gifts turn out to be very ordinary and apparently unspectacular. As Paul emphasized, the Christian body needs a wide variety of members and gifts if it is to function (1 Corinthians 12:12-31). It's not up to us to ask why we have a certain gift, whatever it may be: the important thing is to ask what we can do with it in service of the gospel. It's not what you have that matters—it's what you let God do with it. What you are is God's gift to you; what you become is your gift to God.

God's gifts are given in order to be used. You shouldn't think of God's gifts as some kind of ornament, there just to decorate you and make you a more interesting person. They are there to be used in building up the people of God and furthering his kingdom.

In the parable, the returning master was furious with the servant who buried his talent and refused to use it. Some Christians adopt this ostrich-like approach to their gifts and talents, ignoring them or failing to use them. An English writer of the nineteenth century, John Henry Newman, suggested that each of us should think of ourselves as having to do something for God that nobody else can do. This is a very helpful thought. Identifying what gifts and talents we might have is one of the first steps in finding out what this something might be. And being prepared to use those gifts is essential! They are task-oriented, there for a purpose. They are all on loan. We are responsible for expending them in the world, and we will be held accountable for the way we use them.

God's gifts increase through being used. The parable tells of three servants, two of whom use their talents and the third who buries it in the ground. This final talent remains unaltered in its hole in the ground. It was not used and therefore did not grow. The two other servants, however, found that the money which they had been entrusted with increased through being used wisely. And so it is with the gifts God gives us—gifts such as faith itself. Faith increases through being used, through being put into action in God's service. Faith does not deepen through being allowed to stagnate, but through being applied.

In this respect, doubt is a positive thing. It is a stimulus to growth in faith. It snaps us out of complacency. Like an alarm bell, it indicates that all is not well. Perhaps we have been like the third servant and buried our faith in a hole in the ground, failing to use it. Faith, like a plant, is something meant to grow. So use your faith. Allow it to affect the way you think and the way you live. Don't let it get neglected through disuse!

I'M A FAILURE: WHAT USE CAN I BE TO GOD?

All of us fail God; not all of us, however, are willing to admit this. So let's begin on a positive note: your sense of failure points to your honesty and insight. C. S. Lewis once drew attention to one of the greatest paradoxes of human existence. We have enormously high ideals, which we fail to meet. Knowing what is right and good, we seem unable to achieve these ideals. Many Christians find this paradox expressed in their lives: the deeper their faith, the greater their realization of their sinfulness and inadequacy. As a result, the closer they come to God, the further they feel from him. The more they become aware of the overwhelming love of God for them, the more they realize just how little they love God in return. A sense of inadequacy and failure often arises from a deep awareness of the holiness and righteousness of the God who has called us, which impresses on us the enormity of the moral gulf between ourselves and God. But this isn't really a sense of failure; if anything, it's a proper sense of perspective.

Worldly success. It is certainly true that many Christians are failures by the standards of the world. Paul made this point forcefully when writing to the Corinthian church:

> Consider your own call, brothers and sisters: not many of you were wise by human standards, not many were powerful, not many were of noble birth. But God chose what is foolish in the world to shame the wise; God chose what is weak in the world to shame the strong. (1 Corinthians 1:26-27)

Success in the world usually comes by being aggressive, by ensuring that you come out on top in any conflict and by destroying the reputations of your opponents. Wealth and power are seen as reasonable goals. The weak are legitimate victims to the strong.

The gospel, however, specifies a somewhat different lifestyle, a lifestyle that seems sheer stupidity to those who judge by worldly standards. Great stress is placed on care and compassion for others, especially the weak. Selfish attitudes and behavior are discouraged. The well-being of others is placed above personal success. It is impossible to read the Sermon on the Mount (Matthew 5—7) and avoid seeing areas of serious conflict between Christ's teaching and modern Western business and social ethics.

I was once traveling from London to Geneva in Switzerland and found myself having to spend a long time at London's Heathrow Airport. The flight had been delayed because of fog. I must admit that I find airports rather boring places, and to relieve my boredom, I picked up a copy of the local airport magazine. One of its articles fascinated me: "How You Can Become a Successful Business Executive!" I sat down to read it. It was mainly about how to develop manipulative techniques and project the image of domination and competence. Part of the article was a questionnaire: "When you are in a meeting, what is your aim in reaching a decision?" I looked at the various options and circled "to reach the decision which benefits most people." The right answer was "to come out on top." After awhile, I began to realize that I just didn't have what it took to be a successful business executive—and felt really glad that I didn't! A really successful and powerful business executive or corporate lawyer may seem to have conquered the world—when in reality he or she has been conquered by the world.

Many Christians unwittingly carry over these secular standards of success into their lives as believers after their conversion. They still think of "success" in terms laid down by the world. *Success* means an ability to dominate and manipulate others, to get to the top by every means available, to have status and power. As a result, it is hardly surprising that the people still living by these standards judge themselves and many other Christians to be failures! But what standards are being used here? The gospel challenges the values of the world. It affirms the existence and importance of a different set of values—the values of the kingdom of God. These values are reflected in the lives of Christians, who will inevitably find themselves in tension with at least some of the standards and values of the world. The world says: "seek money, status and possessions." The gospel says: "seek first the kingdom of God" (Matthew 6:33). To become a Christian is to adopt a new lifestyle and set of values, which the world may well brand as a failure. But does what the world thinks really matter?

Failing God. Some Christians, however, are acutely aware of having failed God on some specific occasion, or even a whole series of occasions. Perhaps you feel guilty because you know you could have served God better than you did. Perhaps you failed to speak to someone about the gospel. Perhaps you hurt a friend because of what you said or did. Perhaps you did something that you know to have been wrong. You feel that you are a failure in God's sight. What could he conceivably do through you?

The answer is quite simple: a lot! The classic example of a failure is Peter. Peter, remember, was the disciple who utterly failed Jesus when the going got really tough. In Gethsemane, Peter had affirmed that he would never let Jesus down. "Even though I must die with you, I will not deny you" (Matthew 26:35). Brave words—but, as events showed, hollow ones. Shortly afterward, when Jesus had been arrested, Peter was approached by a servant girl in the high priest's courtyard. "You also were with Jesus the Galilean," she said. Here was an opportunity for Peter to witness to his loyalty to Jesus. However, Peter panicked. If words ever amounted to an admission of total failure, those words were Peter's. "I do not know the man!" (Matthew 26:69-75).

Yet at the heart of the gospel are the themes of forgiveness and renewal. God forgives our past failings and empowers us to start afresh. Martin Luther once described the Christian life as "a kind of beginning all over again." The past is set behind us, as God forgives us for our past failings and empowers us to overcome them in the future. After the resurrection of Jesus, Peter became a changed man. No longer was he a coward who sought to deny Jesus but a potential martyr who was prepared to proclaim his savior to the ends of the earth. It is generally thought that Peter was finally crucified at Rome during the Neronian persecutions in A.D. 65, finally and triumphantly sharing the fate of his Lord.

See your own failings reflected in light of Peter's. Perhaps you thought you could cope with the pressures of a situation, only to discover that you couldn't, and you felt that you let the Lord down. It's not the first time it has happened to someone. Peter must have felt much the same way as you: he was reduced to tears when he realized what a failure he had been (Matthew 26:75). But that was not the end of the story of Peter, nor should it be the end of your story. If you feel that you have let God down, tell him so. Take it to him in prayer. "Trust the past to the mercy of God," writes St. Augustine, "the present to his love, the future to his providence." There is no need to tell anyone else. Remember that God already knows what you have done and how you feel about it (Psalm 139:1-6), so you don't need to hide your fears and anxieties from him. Ask him for forgiveness and for wisdom and strength to cope with such situations in the future. And when you get off your knees, do so with the confidence of one who has been forgiven, ready to face the challenges and opportunities awaiting you.

For all their unfaithfulness and imperfection, God is willing to use his people and to do great things through them. Indeed, it is hard to say which is more remarkable—that people should be so unfaithful or that God should be able to work so marvelously through their unfaithfulness. The sinfulness and pettiness of individuals, the blind selfishness of the churches, the miserliness of the support that they have given to the work of the gospel, the mistakes that have been made—all point to the weakness and failure of people like us. And yet the church survives, the body of Christ in every land, the great miracle of history, in which the living God himself through his Holy Spirit is pleased to dwell. God is able to work through human failures, including yours. Indeed, failure makes us less likely to trust in our own judgment and abilities, and instead to rely on the Lord. This insight is central to Paul's understanding of our life as Christians. "[God] said to me, 'My grace is sufficient for you, for power is made perfect in weakness.' So, I will boast all the more gladly of my weaknesses, so that the power of Christ may dwell in me" (2 Corinthians 12:9).

So don't be anxious if you feel that you are a failure, or that you are totally inadequate as a Christian. The real problems start if you think you're a success, or if you begin to think you're capable of leading a brilliantly successful Christian life trusting in your own strength. The God who has called you is a God who makes his strength perfect through human weakness. Let's be honest: we're all failures when it comes to being Christians. That's why it's such wonderful news that God is able to work through (even despite!) our failures, comforting and reassuring us, before sending us out to try again.

8

DOUBTS ABOUT JESUS CHRIST

Doubts about Jesus tend to be very factual. Every now and then, television or radio features appear which claim to have radical new evidence that totally discredits the Christian understanding of Jesus. Pseudohistorical novels like *The Da Vinci Code* lead their more uncritical readers to believe that they are telling the truth about history, when they are just fiction. The more sensational, the better the book sells. Such sensationalist items may help attract large audiences; nevertheless, their scholarly content is generally low, and their alleged conclusions forgotten within weeks. Some Christians, however, find serious doubts raised in their minds. They do not have access to the scholarly material on which these programs claim to be based and so tend to treat their claims as credible. This chapter deals with the main doubts that are likely to arise in relation to the history of Jesus.

HAVE CHRISTIANS GOT JESUS WRONG?

A number of doubts might arise in this context. Very often books are published with sensational phrases attached to their titles—"the explosively controversial international bestseller," for example—which claim to have recovered "suppressed evidence" con-

cerning Jesus. Earlier Christians, these books allege, hushed facts
about Jesus that didn't fit with their ideas. Sometimes these claims
cause Christians anxiety; however, as I hope to show, these are
needless.

One such doubt might concern whether Jesus really existed,
when in fact the grounds for suggesting that he did not are aston-
ishingly flimsy. Only people who have already made up their
minds that Jesus did not exist as a historical individual could approach the evidence and come to the conclusion that he did not
exist. If the existence of Jesus is supposedly denied on the basis of
the evidence available, we would be obliged to deny the existence
of an alarming number of historical individuals! Although doubts
may be raised on this matter by your friends, or hostile critics of
Christianity, the evidence is strongly against them.

An example of this type of challenge is a book written by John
Allegro, a hitherto respected scholar who argued that the word
Jesus was nothing more and nothing less than some sort of code-
word for a sacred mushroom, which produced hallucinations in
those who consumed them. The early Christians, he argued, far
from being worshipers of the person Jesus Christ, were secret
mushroom-eaters.

The evidence brought forward was quite inadequate. Apart
from destroying Allegro's reputation as a serious scholar, the book
pointed to how easy it is to gain public attention for a theory that
suggests Jesus isn't what Christians have claimed him to be. This
book also showed how difficult it is to draw attention to Christians' refutation of such theories. To claim to have sensational new
evidence to disprove Christianity generates a lot of publicity and
helps sell the book or advertising space on the television feature in
question. But the Christian side of the argument is generally not

heard because it lacks novelty value. It's not newsworthy.

The suggestion that Christianity may have gotten Jesus wrong has been thoroughly explored over the last two hundred years. Just about every possibility has been given careful weight. Jesus might have been a radical vegetarian, a failed revolutionary, a misguided prophet or perhaps nothing more than a religious teacher of common sense. The first Christians might even have deliberately distorted him at points. All these possibilities have been given careful scholarly consideration, yet none has been shown to have any real plausibility.

In the nineteenth century, a movement known as the "Quest of the Historical Jesus" got under way, aiming to show that the New Testament suppressed a true picture of Jesus, but one that Christians didn't like. Although this movement can still be detected today, it has lost most of its intellectual credibility. It has been given full scholarly attention—and then found wanting. Behind these allegedly historical "reconstructions" of Jesus, a web of questionable historical scholarship and vested interests can be detected. "Rediscovered Jesuses" tend to look remarkably like their rediscoverers! In his essay "Fern-Seed and Elephants," C. S. Lewis writes as follows on "rediscovered Jesuses":

> All theology of the liberal type involves at some point—and very often involves throughout—the claim that the real behaviour and purpose and teaching of Christ came very rapidly to be misunderstood and misrepresented by his followers, and has been recovered or exhumed only by modern scholars. Now long before I became interested in theology I had met this kind of theory elsewhere. . . . One was brought up to believe that the real meaning of Plato had been

misunderstood by Aristotle, and wildly travestied by the neo-Platonists, only to be recovered by the moderns. When recovered, it turned out (most fortunately) that Plato had really all along been an English Hegelian, rather like T. H. Green. I have met it a third time in my own professional studies; every week or so a clever undergraduate, every quarter a dull American don, discovers for the first time what some Shakespearian play *really* meant.

IS THE RESURRECTION SOME SORT OF COVER-UP?

One doubt that often arises is whether the resurrection really happened or whether it was some kind of cover-up to conceal the real fate of Jesus. This suggestion was made by skeptics in the first century, frequently in the eighteenth century, and is still encountered today. Doubts about the resurrection arise from suggestions—along with the deep-down feeling of some Christians—that the resurrection is just too good to be true!

For example, some Christians experience anxiety over the resurrection because they think they can't rely on the early Christians' account of what happened. These Christians think: *It was easy for the first Christians to believe in the resurrection of Jesus. After all, belief in resurrections was somewhat commonplace at the time. The first Christians may have jumped to the conclusion that Jesus was raised from the dead when something rather different actually happened.* In fact, however, neither of the two contemporary beliefs of the time bear any resemblance to Christians' claim of how Jesus' resurrection really went. While the Sadducees denied the idea of a resurrection altogether (a fact Paul was able to exploit at an awkward moment: Acts 23:6-8), the majority expectation was of a general resurrection on the last day, at the end of history itself. Being immediately resurrected from the dead was not a common belief or occurrence!

The sheer oddness of the Christian proclamation of the resurrection of Jesus in human history, at a definite time and place, is all too easily overlooked today, even though it was obvious at the time. The unthinkable appeared to have happened and, for that very reason, demanded careful attention. Far from merely fitting into the popular expectation of the pattern of resurrection, what happened to Jesus actually contradicted it. The sheer novelty of the Christian position at the time has been obscured by two thousand years' experience of the Christian understanding of the resurrection. We've gotten used to the idea of Jesus being raised from the dead—yet at the time it was wildly unorthodox and radical. The resurrection of Jesus simply did not conform to contemporary expectations. It wasn't what was expected at all. In fact, so strange is that idea that the early Christians had to give a convincing explanation to account for it.

Of course, some critics have suggested, on Freudian grounds, that the resurrection of Jesus is explicable as some kind of wish-fulfillment on the part of the disciples. This also strains the imagination somewhat. Why should the disciples have responded to the catastrophe of Jesus' death by making the hitherto unprecedented suggestion that God had raised him from the dead? The history of Israel is littered with the corpses of pious Jewish martyrs, none of whom were ever thought of as having been raised from the dead in such a manner. Furthermore, many of the disciples (such as Peter and Paul) appear to have been martyred for their faith: why die for a lie?

Facts about the resurrection. If you are anxious about the resurrection, you may find some of the following points helpful. They by no means exhaust the evidence for the resurrection (further helpful works are listed at the end of the chapter). Nevertheless, they are useful pointers to guide your thinking.

The tomb was empty. Note the emphasis on the historical fact, common to all four Gospels: the tomb was empty (Matthew 28:1-10; Mark 16:1-8; Luke 24:1-11; John 20:1-9). This doesn't prove the resurrection—but it is consistent with it. The Gospels build an overall picture of the events of the first Easter Day, each of which falls into place like a piece in a jigsaw puzzle—consistent with the others, giving a total picture of what happened.

His tomb wasn't venerated. The practice of "tomb veneration" was common in New Testament times. In other words, the tomb of a prophet was used by his disciples as a place of worship. Matthew 23:29-30 almost certainly refers to this practice, which continues to this day: the tomb of David in Jerusalem is still venerated by many Jews. But there is no record whatsoever of any such veneration of the tomb of Jesus by his disciples. Why not? The simple fact was that Jesus' body was disquietingly missing from its tomb.

There seems to have been no dispute about this at the time. The rumor of Jesus' resurrection could have been suppressed without the slightest difficulty by the authorities simply by publicly displaying the corpse of Jesus. It is of greatest importance that the New Testament does not contain as much as a hint of any attempt to explain away the existence of the corpse of Jesus. Nor is there any hint that the Jewish authorities either produced, or attempted to produce, this corpse. Had the corpse been produced, the preaching of the early church would have been discredited immediately. But it wasn't. All the evidence indicates that the tomb was empty on the third day. The controversy at the time concerned not the fact of the empty tomb but the explanation of that emptiness.

His name was exalted. Within a very short period of his death, Jesus was being described in remarkably exalted terms by his followers. Jesus was not venerated as a dead prophet or rabbi but was worshiped as the living and risen Lord. At some points in the New Testament, Jesus appears to be explicitly identified with God himself. At several points in the New Testament, words originally referring to God himself are applied to Jesus. For example, in Romans 10:13, Paul quotes that "everyone who calls upon the name of the Lord [Jesus] will be saved"—yet the original of this Old Testament quotation (Joel 2:32) is actually a statement to the effect that everyone who calls on the name of God will be saved.

How could this remarkable transformation in the perceived status of Jesus have come about if he had remained dead? He died as a common criminal, perhaps even a prophet, or maybe a martyr—but the most this would merit would be veneration of his tomb (see Matthew 23:29). Why did the early Christians start talking about a dead rabbi as if he were God? And, perhaps even more intriguing, why did they start talking about him as if he were alive, praying to him and worshiping him? Once more, the resurrection fits this general pattern. Taken on its own, it proves little; taken in conjunction with all the other pointers, it helps build up a consistent and convincing picture of the resurrection event.

How Can Someone Who Lived Two Thousand Years Ago Be Relevant to Me?

The question of Jesus' ongoing relevance causes difficulty and anxiety for some Christians. To deal with this anxiety, think of Jesus as an event, rather than just a person. Something happened through Jesus. God made something possible through Jesus. Think of Jesus as establishing the grounds of a renewed relationship with God, a new attitude to life, a new hope in the face of death. Or think of him as opening up the way home to God. For, in dealing with Jesus, we aren't dealing simply with a human being like ourselves, but we are dealing with God himself, acting in history to redeem us. God chose to act through Jesus Christ, supremely through his death and resurrection, making available to us something that otherwise would not have been open to us. I sense this excitement in the opening of 1 Peter: "Blessed be the God and Father of our Lord Jesus Christ! By his great mercy he has given us new birth into a living hope through the resurrection of Jesus Christ from the dead, and into an inheritance that is imperishable, undefiled, and unfading, kept in heaven for you" (1 Peter 1:3-4).

First, then, Jesus is of importance to the Christian faith in that, through his death and resurrection, he made possible a whole new way of living. Jesus is the ground of faith: it is because of his obedience to the will of his father—supremely demonstrated in his suffering and death on the cross—that our new relationship to God is possible. The cross is not just an event in history that took place some two thousand years ago; it is the ground of our faith now. It is through the death of Jesus Christ that our new life is possible. "He himself bore our sins in his body on the cross, so that, free from sins, we might live for righteousness; by his wounds you have been healed" (1 Peter 2:24). Without the achievement of the cross, redemption would not be a present possibility for us. Jesus is important because God achieves the salvation of sinful humanity through him. He is the agent of salvation, the one through whom God worked and still works.

Second, Jesus prompts people to ask questions, to begin thinking about God and themselves. Jesus once asked the disciples,

"Who do you say that I am?" (Mark 8:29). That same question has caused many to ponder and wonder ever since. For Christianity is not merely the teachings of Jesus, as Marxism is based on the views of Karl Marx or Thatcherism on those of Margaret Thatcher. The gospel is not just about Jesus; it *is* Jesus. Christianity isn't just about ideas; it is about a person. For many people who subsequently become Christians, Jesus acts as a catalyst or a stimulant to their thinking. The long chain of thought, which climaxes in repentance and acceptance of forgiveness, often begins with interest in the person of Jesus.

There is something strangely attractive about Jesus, something that is able to reach across the gulf of history and intrigue people even today. Questions about Jesus soon become questions about God and salvation. "Who is Jesus?" easily becomes "How can I find a gracious God?" "Why did Jesus have to die?" gives way to "What must I do to be saved?" Interest in Jesus as a person is often the beginning of a long and secret process of reflection, which eventually culminates in acceptance of him as Lord and Savior.

Finally, Jesus indicates what the redeemed life is like. Not only is he the ground or foundation of the life of faith; by his life, he shows us what shape or form the Christian life takes. He maps out a way of living appropriate for believers. His teaching points to the need to value God, to obey him and to ensure that nothing comes before him. By his example he helps us understand what obedience to God implies. He acts as a model for the sort of love that Christians should show to one another. Writing to the Thessalonian Christians, Paul speaks of how, through their conversion, they "became imitators of us and of the Lord" (1 Thessalonians 1:6). Being a Christian means being "conformed to the image of [God's] Son" (Romans 8:29), a process in which God graciously makes us more like Jesus as we deepen in our faith and obedience.

So the fact that Jesus lived two thousand years ago does not diminish his relevance to the life of faith. Without what Jesus achieved, that life and all that it implies would not be possible. Our faith, our hope, all that matters to us—these are all the consequences of what God achieved for us through Jesus. The fact that this new life is a present possibility for others rests on the solid foundation of Jesus Christ. In evangelism we proclaim that the death and resurrection of Jesus make possible and make available a new way of living, a way of living charged with the knowledge of forgiveness and the hope of resurrection and eternal life. That process may be described as "being conformed to Christ," so that we become more like him in the way we behave. Both the foundation and the shape of the redeemed life are built on Jesus—both in New Testament times and today. Through the power of the Holy Spirit, God conforms us to the likeness of his Son, who lives and reigns within us—not as one from the dim and distant past, but as the risen and present Lord.

9

DOUBTS ABOUT GOD

We now turn to consider some anxieties about God. In an aggressively secular society, such as Western Europe or North America, it is very easy for a Christian—especially one who has come to faith recently—to feel threatened and insecure. Is God really there, when so many people deny his existence? Is my faith based on a delusion or a logical error? Unease over such questions is natural, and I hope that the response given here is helpful.

Anxieties about God, however, concern more than his existence. Is he faithful to his promises? Does he really love me, a sinner? These questions trouble many Christians, especially when they go through some kind of spiritual dry patch (quite a common occurrence, by the way; cf. Psalm 63:1). Although we have already looked at some doubts about God (for example, when you don't experience God as being present in your life), the additional material presented here should help you think and pray through your worries.

IS GOD REALLY THERE?

As I mentioned earlier, there are no knock-down arguments that irrefutably establish God's existence, just as there are none that decisively disprove it. Whether people believe or disbelieve in God, their position is a matter of faith, not fact. It may be a fact that God is an irrelevance to many individuals, just as it may be a fact that many people do not believe in God—but this does not mean that it is a fact that God does not exist.

But faith in God doesn't depend on an argument anyway. The Austrian philosopher Ludwig Wittgenstein remarked that he'd never met anyone who came to faith in God on account of an argument! Rather, arguments for God's existence are developed as back-up defenses for the gospel, for the benefit of those who think this is important. Some people need to be reassured that Christianity makes sense; arguments for the existence of God show that a rational case can indeed be made for belief in him. Although God's existence doesn't depend on those arguments, it can be helpful to know that a case can be made for it.

In the end, however, we know that God exists (and who and what he is) because he has revealed himself. Arguments for the existence of God may help prepare the way for this revelation (Romans 1:18-20), but they are no substitute for it. If Christianity was about our search for God, there would be permanent difficulties in agreeing on who or what God was, let alone whether he existed. Different search parties would come back from their expeditions with differing reports, unable to reach agreement on their results.

Christianity, however, affirms that God has come looking for us. His existence is disclosed by his search for us and, ultimately, by his encounter with us. C. S. Lewis wrote powerfully of the profound silliness of the idea of "our search for God" in his work *Miracles*:

> The Pantheist's God does nothing, demands nothing. He is there if you wish for him, like a book on a shelf. He will not

pursue you. . . . The shock comes at the precise moment when the thrill of life is communicated to us along the clue we have been following. It is always shocking to meet life when we thought we were alone. . . . And therefore this is the very point at which many draw back—I would have done so myself if I could—and proceed no further with Christianity. An "impersonal God"—well and good. A subjective God of beauty, truth and goodness, inside our own heads—better still. A formless life-force surging through us, a vast power which we can tap—best of all. But God himself, alive, pulling at the other end of the cord, perhaps approaching at infinite speed, the hunter, king, husband—that is quite another matter. There comes a moment when the children who have been playing at burglars hush suddenly: was that a real footstep in the hall? There comes a moment when people who have been dabbling in religion ("Man's search for God"!) suddenly draw back. Supposing we really found him? We never meant to come to that! Worse still supposing he had found us?

In his autobiography *Surprised by Joy,* Lewis further suggests that our alleged search for God is rather like the mouse who went out looking for the cat. "It is a fearful thing to fall into the hands of the living God" (Hebrews 10:31)—it demands obedience, conversion and newness of life!

For many Christians, the sudden conversion of their friends (or even their own conversion) points to the existence of God. An individual who, up to that point, has been hostile to God suddenly changes. God suddenly becomes both meaningful and present to them. Something has happened. But what? And how? Through-

out, Scripture bristles with ideas and images that help illuminate
this event, all pointing to the idea of an active God who discloses
his existence, not through argument but through action. The con-
frontation with Saul of Tarsus is perhaps the classic example of
this. God suddenly became real in Saul's, and our, experience.

It is interesting to notice that no biblical writer ever feels the
need to prove the existence of God. That God is there is taken for
granted. How could anyone think he wasn't? He was experienced
and encountered; he made demands of individuals and communities; he promised to be with his people, wherever they went. Thus
the resurrection of Jesus is not taken by New Testament writers as
proof of the existence of God, but it is interpreted as assigning
Jesus a status equal with that of God. It is very difficult for someone who has experienced the power and presence of God to doubt
that God exists.

IS GOD FAITHFUL TO HIS PROMISES?

Both the Old and New Testaments affirm that God makes promises to us. Many of these promises are powerful and deeply moving. The great promise of God to Joshua is an inspiration to many
Christians: "Be strong and courageous; do not be frightened or dismayed, for the LORD your God is with you wherever you go"
(Joshua 1:9). As Christians we must learn to trust in the gracious
promises of God, promises such as that made to Joshua and,
through him, to us. But how reliable are these promises? How
trustworthy is God? Christianity lays great stress on the total truthfulness and trustworthiness of God—but how well placed is this
trust? Is God faithful to his promises?

This question is one that perplexed many Jews shortly before
the time of Jesus. God had promised them a messiah. He had

promised to come to his temple. He had promised to send his messenger before him to prepare the way for his coming (e.g., Malachi 3:1). But nothing had happened. Judea was under Roman occupation. Prophecy had died out. The word of the Lord was heard rarely in the land (as in the days of Eli; see 1 Samuel 3:1). It seemed as if the great promises of God would come to nothing.

Then John the Baptist appeared in the country around Judea (Mark 1:1-8). It is difficult for the modern reader to understand the sense of excitement and expectation that this aroused. John was dressed like Elijah (Mark 1:6; cf., 2 Kings 1:8), the greatest of the prophets. He spoke with authority and proclaimed that he had come to prepare the way for the coming of God to his people. How the Old Testament prophecies must have come to life again as people swarmed across the Judean countryside to hear this remarkable man and speculate about who would follow him. Whose way had he prepared?

I remember once having to spend a damp winter Sunday afternoon waiting for a train to arrive at the Nottingham station, in the English east midlands. My wife and son had been to visit relatives in Chester and were returning that afternoon. The train was due to arrive at 3:30 p.m. My faith in British railways has never been especially great, and it was lowered still further that afternoon. By 4:10 p.m., the train had still not arrived. Eventually, there was an announcement. A rather despondent, disembodied female voice told us that British Rail regretted that the train had been delayed, but it should arrive in twenty minutes. I, and about fifty others, waited twenty minutes. It got dark, and the mist from the nearby canal enveloped the platform. People began to huddle up against each other for warmth. Nothing happened. Ten minutes later, another announcement was made. A decidedly gloomy voice told us that British Rail was very sorry, but there would be a delay of at least half an hour before the train arrived. The train was definitely on its way, but all sorts of problems had developed along the line. Finally, at 5:55 p.m., a decidedly more cheerful female voice announced that the train now approaching platform five was the delayed train from Chester. In other words, it had been sighted, and at any moment it would pull into the station. A cheer went up from the waiting crowd, who clearly shared my frustration at having to spend the best part of a miserable Sunday afternoon in this way.

I imagine Israel felt much the same relief when John the Baptist appeared. He was like the voice who announced that a delayed train was just about to arrive. Something was happening, and things were on the move. The long-awaited arrival of the Messiah was imminent. And just as the small crowd of us surged to the edge of the platform to catch a glimpse of the incoming train, so the Jews streamed out into the countryside to catch a glimpse of the long-awaited Messiah.

For the New Testament writers, the coming of God's Messiah to his people is one of the best demonstrations of God's faithfulness to his promises. For example, it's very difficult to read Matthew's gospel and miss his excitement at pointing out how great Old Testament prophecies found their fulfillment in Jesus. The same sort of excitement, even relief, can be seen in Simeon's overjoyed reaction at seeing Jesus: at last, everything I have waited for from the Lord has come to pass! Now I can die in peace of mind (Luke 2:28-32). God had faithfully fulfilled his promises to his people.

For Paul, the faithfulness of God was of central importance. This faithfulness is demonstrated in the life, death and resurrection of Jesus, in which the promises of the Old Testament were taken up and fulfilled. "For in him every one of God's promises is a 'Yes' " (2 Corinthians 1:20). The coming of Christ is seen as the fulfillment of the great Old Testament prophecies of God's coming to dwell among his people (Malachi 3:1-4; Luke 2:25-30), just as the resurrection is seen as a fulfillment of God's promise of redemption (1 Corinthians 15:4). And on the basis of that faithfulness to his past promises, we may trust those promises that still await their fulfillment—the great New Testament promises of renewal and eternal life.

It's helpful to think about the faith of the Old Testament saints at this point. They trusted passionately in the power of the Lord to redeem them. Yet, until the coming of Jesus Christ, the great divine promises of redemption seemed unfulfilled. But we can look back on the Old Testament period and see how those great promises were fulfilled through the coming of Jesus. In his life, death and his resurrection, Jesus demonstrated God's faithfulness to his promises. It's much easier for us to believe in the promises of God than it was for the Old Testament saints—they never got to see those promises fulfilled in Jesus! Through Jesus, "we have the prophetic message more fully confirmed" (2 Peter 1:19): in other words, the great promises of the Old Testament are made more credible by the coming of Jesus.

One of the most powerful passages in the New Testament describes the nature of faith in God (Hebrews 11:1—12:3). In this passage we are reminded of the deeds of many of the great figures of the Old Testament. Their faith in God and his gracious promises is shown in their actions. Abraham trusted in God and left his native land to go to the land chosen by God. Moses left Egypt in faith, trusting in the great promise of delivery from bondage and entry into the Promised Land. And in these promises, the coming of Christ to redeem his people was anticipated. None of these great Old Testament believers saw the coming of Jesus—yet they placed their faith in the promises of God. "All of these died in faith without having received the promises, but from a distance they saw and greeted them" (Hebrews 11:13). Yet we have received what was promised to them—the coming of the redeemer, Jesus Christ. We share their faith in the same God, but we can have greater confidence in his promises, in the light of their confirmation through the coming of Jesus.

Perhaps more important, consider what we know about the character and purpose of God, as we know it through the death of Jesus Christ on the cruel cross of Calvary for our salvation. In the death of Jesus on that cross, we learn that God loves sinners such as ourselves, that he is committed to the cause of our redemption. God shows his love for us, in that Christ died for us while we were still sinners (Romans 5:8). This is the God with whom we are dealing—the God who has given everything at his disposal to demonstrate his astonishing love for us and bring us back to him. It is simply inconceivable that God, having invested so much in our well-being and care, having committed himself to us in word and deed, should abandon us or fail to be faithful to us. The cross of Christ demonstrates the vital fact that God stands by his promises, whatever the cost to himself, asking us to accept them, trust them and thus to enter into eternal life with him—something which nothing, not even the very gates of hell themselves, can tear away from us.

God is working his purpose out—and part of that purpose is the salvation of sinful human beings, people like you and me. If God is on our side, who can be against us? Or, as the motto of Oxford University has it, quoting Psalm 27:1, "The Lord is my light and my salvation; whom shall I fear? The Lord is the stronghold of my life; of whom shall I be afraid?" Remind yourself of the words of reassurance spoken by Jesus to Nicodemus: "God so loved the world that he gave his only Son, so that everyone who believes in him may not perish but may have eternal life" (John 3:16). You may be reassured that God loves you, and that by putting your trust in him, you enter into a relationship with him. The gospel is not about an easy ride through life; it makes hard and difficult demands of us. But it also makes us a promise—the promise of the presence and comfort of God as we seek to do his will in his world. And the comfort of knowing that God stands by us, even in our darkest hours, is more than I can ever hope to convey in print.

HOW CAN I KNOW THAT GOD LOVES ME?

A question that has troubled many Christians, especially those who are intensely aware of their own sinfulness, is "How can I know that God loves me?" Somehow it seems that God can love us only if he ignores our sin or pretends that we aren't really sinners after all. Experience, conscience and faith seem to be out of step here! How can God love people like us?

Much the same point is made by Paul. It's conceivable to imagine circumstances under which you might give your life for somebody else. Of course, it would have to be somebody rather splendid, a really good person. Even then, however, it would still be unusual for someone to die for another person. Yet God demonstrates his love for us, in that Christ died for us while we were still sinners (Romans 5:6-8). What on earth would he do that for? Why should God love sinners so much? Even before we got around to repenting, God loved us. Amazingly, God loved us long before we loved him (1 John 4:10-11).

Our disbelief that God should love us ultimately rests on our feeling that God's love must depend on our attractiveness. We find it difficult to see anything special about ourselves that should merit so astonishing and so loving a response from God. But God's love for us ultimately rests on his own character. We have the privilege of being made in his image (Genesis 1:26-27). The cross of Christ expresses the nature and the full extent of the tender love of God for us, assuring us of how precious we are in his sight. How often has it been said that "beauty is in the eye of the beholder"? Why should God see us as worthy of his love? Not because of anything that we have done, or anything that we are, but because of what God is like—and what he has done for us through Jesus Christ.

In part, our difficulty in accepting that God loves us arises from a sense of sin. Most of us feel profoundly unworthy of the love of God because of our selfishness and guilt. Sin affects us profoundly in what we think, say and do. It makes us tend to be skeptical about God, disobedient to him and reluctant to trust him. Yet God is able to distinguish between sin and the sinner. Sin is like a force that holds us in captivity against our will; God sees us as captives, struggling to escape, and takes pity on us. It is like rust, which distorts the image of God within us; God anticipates the renewal and restoration of that image. Sin is like a wound which disfigures us; God looks forward to the time when we will, through his grace, be healed. Sin is like a layer of dirt or corrosion which makes us seem unattractive and unbecoming; God sees us as washed clean, our beauty restored to what it was on the first morning of creation.

An illustration might be helpful here. In the late fifteenth century, the Florentine sculptor Agostino d'Antonio began work on a huge block of marble, with a view to producing a spectacular sculpture. After a few attempts to make something out of it, he gave it up as worthless. The block of marble—now badly disfigured—lay idle for forty years. Then Michelangelo took an interest in it. He saw beyond the ugly disfigured block of marble to the magnificent artistic creation he knew he could achieve with it. As a result, he began work. The final statue—the celebrated David—is widely regarded as one of the most outstanding artistic achievements of all time.

Michelangelo was able to see beyond the ugly exterior of the block of marble to what he could eventually achieve with it. Similarly, God is able to see beyond our sinful predicament and all its consequences, knowing what he will be able to do with us through breaking the power of sin and restoring us to his image and likeness. Christ's atoning death both breaks the power of sin and purges its disfiguring and distorting presence from our lives. Within each of us the image of God (Genesis 1:26-27) is found, however disfigured and corrupted by sin it may presently be. God is able to recover this image through grace, as we are conformed to Christ. Just as the figure of David lay hidden within the marble, discernable only to the eye of its creator, so the image of God (however tarnished by sin) lies within us, seen and known by God himself. Yet God loves us while we are still sinners! He doesn't have to wait until we stop sinning. Acceptance of that love of God for us is a major step along the road that leads to our liberation from the tyranny of sin.

How, finally, can we be reassured of the love of God for us? Perhaps one of the most helpful ways of doing this is to reflect on the image of the dying Christ, stretched out on the cross for us. Try to imagine the scene. Even better, find some paintings of the scene, such as those that have become classics in the history of art. Perhaps you could read one of the four passion narratives (Matthew 27:11-65; Mark 15; Luke 23; John 18:28—19:42) and picture the events of that first Good Friday—so memorably and vividly portrayed in the film *The Passion of the Christ*. Think carefully of the loneliness, pain, suffering, and the sense of hopelessness and helplessness of the scene. Think of that sad and dignified face, contorted with pain. Let the full horror of that scene impress itself on your mind. And all of this because God loved you and gave his only Son for you.

For many Christians, one of the most powerful ways of recalling this scene, and understanding its relevance for us, is to share in a Communion service. The bread and the wine are visible, tangible reminders of that scene. They represent the sufferings of Christ. They are, as Charles Wesley describes them, "dear tokens of his passion." And as you eat and drink the bread and wine, you are being reminded of the enormous cost of your redemption, of how much you must matter to God if he went to such lengths to find you. Let them act as triggers to your memory, starting off trains of thought that can converge on the crucifixion of the Lord. "In this is love, not that we loved God but that he loved us and sent his Son to be the atoning sacrifice for our sins" (1 John 4:10).

An aunt of mine died some time ago, having lived to be eighty or so. She had never married. During the course of clearing out her possessions, we came across a battered old photograph of a young man. My aunt had, it turned out, fallen hopelessly in love as a young girl. It had ended tragically. She never loved anyone else and kept a photograph of the man she had loved for the remainder of her life. Why? Partly to remind herself that she had once been loved by someone. As she had grown old, she knew that she would have difficulty in believing that, at one point in her life, she really had meant something to someone, that someone had once cared for her and regarded her as his everything. It could all have seemed a dream, an illusion, something she had invented in her old age to console her in her declining years—except that the photograph gave the lie to that. It reminded her that it had not been invented; she really loved someone once and was loved in return. The photograph was her sole link with a world in which she had been valued.

The communion bread and wine are like that photograph. They reassure us that something that seems too good to be true—something that we might even be suspected of having invented—really did happen. They are reminders of that day in the past when the Son of God gave himself for us, assuring us that we matter profoundly to God, despite our sin. They are tokens of that precious moment in history when love took on a new meaning and depth. They invite us to remember and cherish—but above all, to be reassured of—the wonderful love of God for sinners like us.

10

DOUBT

How to Handle It

The previous four chapters have dealt with specific doubts and anxieties that cause concern to many Christians. Since this work is likely to be read by many students and young Christians, I have often addressed issues and doubts that may occur in the early stages of growth in faith. But doubt is something that is experienced by all Christians, young and mature. In this chapter I will deal with some more general strategies for coping with doubt throughout the life of faith.

FAITH AND A HOSTILE CULTURE

We noted earlier how our culture seems to encourage doubt. This idea of the hostility of Western culture toward faith is not new. In a BBC radio address in 1942, C. S. Lewis described faith as existing on "enemy territory." Writing during World War II, when much of continental Europe was occupied by Nazi armies, Lewis was trying to express the idea that faith is like a resistance movement that is hostile to the invading power. That invading power is determined to stamp out any resistance it meets.

Since Lewis wrote, Western culture has become much more aggressively secular. Those committed to secular values have a vested interest in destroying the credibility of the Christian faith—and that means your personal faith as well. It is very common for Christians to find themselves isolated at work or ridiculed for their faith. They are very conscious of the fact that their faith marks them out as "abnormal" in the eyes of their colleagues. It's almost as if they have to apologize for believing in God. Christian values and presuppositions are gradually being squeezed out of every area of modern Western culture. Faith, like a resistance movement, has to survive in a very hostile environment. But it *can* survive. Christianity is, as Lewis puts it, "a fighting religion."

Many Christians find the new aggressiveness of secular culture deeply disturbing. It seems to call their faith into question. The hostility of much of Western society seems very threatening. It causes many Christians to become despondent. At best, the world seems indifferent to their faith; at worst, it treats it as absurd. Doubt can thus arise from a sense of bewilderment, of despondency, at the hostility of the world—often including close friends and relatives—to the gospel. How can I believe the gospel when it meets such hostility and aggression?

There are three points to be made here, some academic, some pastoral. But their underlying theme is the same. Western culture is going through a phase which is not just non-Christian but actually anti-Christian. That means we must be realistic about the hostile attitudes against Christianity that we are likely to encounter at every level. It has no bearing on whether Christianity is right or wrong. But it does place us under pressure on account of our faith. So we must be realistic about the origin and purpose of this anti-Christian propaganda and learn to cope with it. With that in mind, let's look at these three points.

Others' ignorance. First, the popular reaction to an idea has no bearing on whether it is true or not. People may ridicule faith in God—but that doesn't mean it is wrong. Most people have little understanding of what Christianity is all about. Very often they reject a caricature of the gospel, not the gospel itself. You may well find that, once you begin to explain what Christians believe (and why they believe it), some of the hostility and lack of understanding begin to disappear. Johann Wolfgang von Goethe put it this way: "We have got used to the fact that people make fun of things they don't understand." It isn't as if everyone has tried Christianity and then decided it is no good. Nor is it as if they've all thought deeply about it and decided it can't be right. Most people give Christianity little thought and very often base even that on misunderstandings. You may find yourself in the privileged position of helping people come to faith by removing their misconceptions and misunderstandings of the gospel.

Perspective. Second, try to think yourself into the situation faced by the first Christians during the New Testament period. They were faced with hostility on every side. They were ridiculed as fools (a very early anti-Christian graffito shows a man kneeling, worshiping a crucified man—with the head of an ass). They were very few in number. There were enormous barriers of culture and language to overcome if the gospel was to be spread. Again, try to think yourself into their situation and imagine how incredibly despondent you might feel about it! Yet the apostles were not unduly worried by these problems. They weren't overwhelmed by the hostility of their environment. The resurrection of Jesus set those difficulties in perspective. The God who raised Jesus from the dead was with them and on their side. And neither should we feel intimidated or threatened. In fact, the new hostility of secular culture to the gospel makes it easier for us to identify with the Christian communities we read about in the New Testament letters. Their situation is very like ours in many respects. So take comfort from the experience of the early Christians, and let yourself be inspired and encouraged by their words and examples.

Support. Third, appreciate the pastoral importance of support groups. Make sure you don't get isolated and have to cope with the pressures placed on you by society on your own. You need to be encouraged by other Christians. You need to spend time with other people whose worldview is the same as yours. This is particularly important for Christian students at a college or university, where pressure from secular beliefs and values can be considerable. The world aims to isolate you, to demoralize you, to break down your confidence in yourself and the gospel (read John 17:14-18). You need to be able to discuss problems you have in common—such as how to cope with the pressure brought on Christians by society in general, by your colleagues at work, or by your family and friends in particular. Doubt can be a symptom of inadequate pastoral support. Don't just go to church—get involved in home groups, Bible study groups, special interest groups, house parties or camps. Encourage your fellow Christians, and let them encourage you.

DON'T GET PREOCCUPIED WITH YOUR DOUBTS

Don't worry too much about doubt! Doubt focuses attention on ourselves and our anxieties and stops us from trusting in God. A preoccupation with doubt is just as pointless as a preoccupation with death: it doesn't change the situation, and it distracts our attention from the opportunities that the life of faith has to offer. Preoccupation with doubt is like constant spiritual introspection in which we spend all our time looking inward at our own feelings and doubts—when we should be looking outward, to the living God who brought our faith into being and has promised to nourish and support that faith through the hard times. Preoccupation with doubt weakens or even cuts the lifeline between us and the living God; it distracts us from our life of prayer and devotion. This sort of preoccupation with doubt paralyzes our spiritual growth. We stagnate through lack of motivation to grow.

Doubt is like an attention-seeking child: when you pay attention to it, it demands that you pay even more attention. This is a vicious circle that is difficult to escape from. If we feed our doubts, they'll grow. Yet doubt can bring home to us just how precious a thing faith is. It brings home how unthinkable life would be without the comforting presence of God. Doubt allows us to step briefly from the world of faith into the world of unbelief and realize how hostile and frightening a place it must be. The grass isn't always greener on the other side of the fence! See doubt instead as an invitation to nourish your faith, and deprive your doubts of the attention they need to grow. View doubt as an opportunity, rather than a problem. See it as an invitation to grow in faith and consolidate your spiritual resources, rather than a sign of decay. Your faith will only decay if you let doubt overwhelm you.

Doubt is also an invitation to spiritual growth, since it can be a sign of a neglected faith—a faith that has been taken for granted and not nourished and allowed to grow. It points to a vulnerable faith. We need to work continually at all our relationships, consolidating and deepening them—and that applies to our relationship with God as well. Doubt may be a sign that we've neglected our relationship with God. It's not the symptom that's important—it's the malaise it might indicate. Doubt signposts the need for spiritual renewal, growth and consolidation. So don't get preoccupied with your doubts; instead, get to work on renewing, deepening and consolidating your faith in God. Just as a person who is undernourished is especially prone to illness, so a neglected and undernourished faith is particularly susceptible to doubt. Prevention, we are told, is better than cure—and this applies to doubt as much as anything else.

It is therefore important to develop strategies that enable your faith to develop. That doesn't mean trying harder to believe; it means allowing your faith to rest on firmer personal and doctrinal foundations. I've already stressed the need to deepen our understanding of Christian doctrine (pp. 27-31): the more we understand our faith, the greater our confidence in its ideas. But what about the personal foundations of faith? What does it mean to develop the "personal foundations" of faith? An exposition of the parable of the sower will help make this important way of coping with doubt clearer.

The parable of the sower. One of the most positive ways of handling doubt is to read the parable of the sower (Mark 4:1-20) and reflect carefully on its implications. It is a powerful parable, vividly conveying some important points. One of its main emphases is the goodness of the seed. Whatever happens to the seed is a result of the ground on which it falls; it does not reflect variable quality in the seed itself. As Jesus stresses, the seed represents the Word of God. The Word of God really is able to effect transformation in our lives. Just as the word of God was able to call creation into existence (Genesis 1:1-27), so the same creative word is able to transform our sinful lives, recreating us after the likeness of God.

But what if we present that seed with unsuitable soil? What if we, by the reception that we give to the seed, make it difficult for it to take root and grow? Doubt can be a symptom of poor soil that has been neglected and starved of nutrients. The parable is an invitation to consider what sort of ground we are providing for the seed—can it grow and flourish? Existing doubt may be overcome, and future doubt made less likely, by allowing the seed of the gospel to grow vigorously in the ground of your life (Hosea 10:12). That ground needs to be tilled and made fertile—something you can do. Considering two different kinds of soil helps to bring this point out clearly.

The seed sown in rocky places (Mark 4:5-6, 16-17). Here, the seed falls on rocky ground. This doesn't mean ground littered with rocks; rather, it means ground with a very thin layer of soil over the solid rock beneath. The seed is able to germinate without difficulty. However, when it tries to take root, there is insufficient earth available. It is unable to develop a root that will enable it to gain access to water and necessary minerals and to be physically stable. As a result, it cannot survive.

Some people develop a very superficial faith in the gospel, which never takes root properly. Often, it is very emotional in character, relying heavily on experience of the presence of God or an unbalanced understanding of the work of the Holy Spirit. While such a faith is initially enormously enthusiastic, it lacks real substance. It is like the house built on sand rather than rock—it lacks a solid foundation, being too dependent on human emotional states and not relying on the promises of God. As a result, this faith is very vulnerable to doubt. The moment God isn't experienced as present, there is a temptation to assume he isn't present at all.

To change this situation we need to replace this rocky ground with good soil, so that the seed may take root. You can do this by relying less on your emotions and feelings, and letting your faith feed on the promises of God. It is very helpful to meditate on the promises of God (e.g., in the Psalms), reflecting on their vitality and relevance. Try to read books that will deepen your understanding of the Christian faith—in other words, which will help you see how solid and substantial Christianity really is. You don't need to read very many, and you don't need to read them very quickly!

Much of the popular literature read by Christians is biographical, about the lives and experiences of Christians. In many ways, of course, this is very helpful. It allows us to see how others have faced challenges similar to our own. It gives us some models for developing our own lifestyle as a Christian. It suggests things that we might not otherwise have thought about. And they're usually easy reading. Despite all these obvious advantages, a serious difficulty remains. Such books may tell us a lot about the people who wrote them or the people who they're about—but they don't necessarily teach us much about God. They don't necessarily deepen our understanding of the Christian faith.

So read those carefully, but also try to spend time developing your understanding and knowledge of the Christian faith. It is by feeding your faith that you can starve your doubts to death. It is by letting your faith grow that your doubts will be choked. How? Some suggestions may prove helpful. Although they are particularly aimed at a student readership, they are of relevance to a much wider audience.

First, read Scripture regularly with a daily study plan. Keep a note of verses that seem helpful or relevant. Try memorizing them. Use a commentary to help you grasp the meaning of passages. And don't allow your study to be of purely academic interest; your faith affects the way you act, your values and aspirations, as well as your ideas. Try to identify areas of your life in which you feel there is room for improvement in the light of your reading of Scripture, and especially your reflections on Jesus himself. Allow faith to become obedience. Allow your head and heart to interact!

And don't get permanently locked into a pattern of Bible reading or prayer that reflects the specific rhythm of student life. You must be prepared to be adaptable. As a student, you may find that you can set aside a period early in the morning or late at night for Bible study and prayer. But what happens if you become a parent and have small children who prevent you getting a good night's sleep? Or what if you enter a career that makes severe demands at just those times you used to set aside for prayer? Be prepared to adapt. Develop new patterns of prayer—if necessary, grabbing time as and when it arises. It is more important to read Scripture and pray than to do these things at a fixed time! Let your prayer pattern be realistic, tailored to your present situation—not what things were like for you ten or twenty years ago.

Also, read some books that will stimulate your thinking about the content of your faith. This will not merely help you develop your own Christian mind, it will give you the resources to help others think through similar questions. One of the most helpful writers with this is C. S. Lewis, now widely regarded as probably the most important popular Christian writer of the twentieth century. *Mere Christianity, The Problem of Pain* and *Miracles* are excellent works with which to begin thinking through a range of important questions. His collection The Chronicles of Narnia, especially *The Lion, The Witch and the Wardrobe,* presents many central Christian ideas in the form of a children's tale, which has become a modern classic. You can cut your theological teeth on these and enjoy yourself at the same time!

If you are experiencing doubt, you will find Lewis's *Screwtape Letters* particularly fascinating. In this book Lewis speculates on the strategies and tactics of a senior and a junior devil, whose task it is to convert you to atheism. You will probably see doubt and temptation in a new light as a result. According to Lewis, doubt is something we must expect to happen. The stronger our faith, the more likely we are to be subjected to attack by doubt. Doubt is part of Screwtape's strategy for paralyzing and crippling our faith and preventing us from being of use to God. Doubt, like temptation, is something Screwtape uses to distance us from God. If insights like this seem helpful, there are many more like them within the pages of *The Screwtape Letters*.

Read some books, as well, that will stimulate your thinking about prayer and Christian devotion. Remember that people have been putting their trust in Jesus Christ for the past two thousand years, and many have written of their experiences in works that have become spiritual classics. Many of these are easy to get hold of. By dipping into them, you can help yourself develop your prayer and devotional life. There are times when many Christians find prayer difficult, or feel that they are going through a spiritual dry patch—a period in which their spiritual life seems dry and parched (see Psalm 63:1; 143:6). If this is your problem, don't accept it passively—use it actively. Let God work through it. Reading classic works about prayer and devotion (an area often referred to as "spirituality") can help you through these difficult periods, as well as providing a great stimulus at other times.

Some examples may prove helpful. In 1418 a book titled *The Imitation of Christ,* written by Thomas à Kempis, began to be read widely and soon became a classic. It is broken down into 114 short chapters—each usually less than a page long, rich in scriptural quotations and allusions, dealing with a single theme (e.g., "Loving Jesus Above All Else," "Close Friends with Jesus," "Humble Obedience After the Example of Jesus Christ" or "Asking God's Help and Being Confident of Regaining His Grace"). Although written by a monk for monks, the book has freshness, profundity and power and has stimulated generations of believers. It is a work you can dip into occasionally or read regularly. As a sample, here are some of his thoughts on doubt, taken from the chapter "How to Resist Temptation":

> The beginning of all evil temptation is an unstable mind and lack of trust in God. Just as a ship without a helm is driven to and fro by the waves, so a careless man, who abandons his proper course, is tempted in countless ways. . . . So we must not despair when we are tempted, but earnestly pray to God to grant us his help in every need. For, as Paul says, "when you are tempted, God will provide a way to overcome it, so that we may be able to bear it." So let us humble ourselves under the hand of God in every trial and difficulty, for he will save and raise up the humble in spirit.

By dipping into works such as these, "useful thoughts for the day" can be gleaned. There are, of course, many other writers in addition to Thomas à Kempis—but he is an excellent starting point for those new to this type of writing. You might also like to try Brother Lawrence's *Practice of the Presence of God*. But remember that spirituality is largely a matter of personal taste! If you don't like a writer, try someone else.

Try keeping a spiritual diary as well, in which you can jot down scriptural references that seem helpful to your needs, or quotations from books you have read that helped you think through a problem or which seemed to cast light on some difficulty. You could just note page references to books if you found whole sections that seemed relevant to your needs. Later, you can read through this book and benefit from your accumulated insights. We all know how very easy it is to forget precisely where a useful passage is found just when you need it most!

The seed sown among thorns (Mark 4:7, 18-19). Some seed fell on ground in which there were other plants (thorns) already growing. There would have been intense competition for water, light and space in which to grow. The problem is well known to every gardener: before planting seed, first get rid of all the weeds! If you don't, they will choke the seed as it attempts to grow. When the seed of the gospel is planted in a person's life, it begins to grow, but that growth can easily be threatened.

Try to imagine how a professional gardener goes about planting valuable seeds. He won't throw them on uncleared ground where other plants can deprive them of the sunlight, warmth and moisture essential to their germination and growth. He'll create the most favorable growing conditions he can, ensuring that nothing will get in the way of his valuable seeds. He will plant them in compost, free from other seeds or plants. He will ensure that they receive warmth, light and adequate water.

If God has planted the seed of the gospel in your heart and mind, it is already growing. You can be assured of that. Now it's up to you to encourage its growth. This means allowing God to work as he uproots thorns and other such plants that will prevent the seed of the gospel from growing properly. If this isn't done, the seed hasn't much of a chance; it will be choked by plants that are already there. Faith cannot grow in this situation and will be exceptionally vulnerable to doubt. To allow faith to grow and develop its resistance to doubt, you must remain in God and allow him to eliminate competition for your heart and mind. You must help it to grow by removing obstacles to that growth.

What sort of obstacles? The parable identifies several: the worries of this life, the lure of wealth and the desire to possess other things (verse 19). Basic human ambition, the desire to be rich and famous, the thirst to outperform our competitors, anxieties about money and status—all these are competing for growing space with the gospel within our lives. To change the image slightly, they are competing for our loyalty. "You cannot serve two masters," such as God and money (Matthew 6:24). This point is made with special clarity in 1 Timothy 6:8-10, which stresses the destructive effects of total dedication to the quest for money.

A faith under such pressure is very vulnerable to doubt. Anxieties about status, security, power or money can easily encroach on our relationship with God. Jesus spoke powerfully of the effects of the cares and anxieties of the world on faith, and he commended studying the birds of the air and the lilies of the field as an example of the tranquility of faith (Matthew 6:25-34). Note the constant stress: Do not worry. Do not be anxious. Trust in God, and all else will fall into perspective. It is by seeking the kingdom of God and his righteousness—rather than worldly status or possessions—that peace of mind and growth in faith comes.

This section of the parable of the sower thus points to a definite course of action on our part. We are being asked to examine ourselves, to ask what our top priorities are. It is very helpful to make a list of the matters uppermost in your mind at the moment, grading them in order of importance. For most of us, drawing up of a list like this is a very revealing affair, bringing home to us how pre-

occupied we are with anxieties and concerns that have no direct
bearing on our Christian life. If we do not look after our faith, can
we be surprised if it falters occasionally? If we direct all our efforts
toward other goals, we have correspondingly less time and incli-
nation to work at our relationship with God. In fact, by concentrating our attention on matters relating to our status, wealth and
power, we are actually encouraging the growth of thorns, which
will choke the seed of the gospel.

Doubt can therefore be a symptom of a neglected faith, a faith
that has been untended and uncared for. Nevertheless, that ne-
glect can be reversed. The thorn bushes that have, up to now, been
choking it can be removed, gradually or immediately. You can take
steps to eliminate the anxieties that so often give rise to doubt. The
first stage in this process is identifying these anxieties and attempt-
ing to trace their causes. You can do this on your own or in con-
sultation with a friend or older Christian. What sort of anxieties
are we talking about?

You can try to answer this question yourself. Write down on a
sheet of paper the thoughts that are uppermost in your mind.
What thoughts are dominant at this moment? Who or what is top
on your list of mental priorities? Most Christians, if they are being
honest, find that God tends to come low down on a list like this.
Other matters assume greater importance. Drawing up this kind
of list is an excellent way of recalling us to God. Yet Martin Luther
once remarked that "where your heart is, and where your security
is, that has become your God." In other words, whatever we give
mental priority to is our God—what a frightening thought! Our
anxieties thus help us see what we treat as being really important
and show us how easy it is to let God slip down our list of priorities.

Your faith affects your everyday life, but your faith is also affected by everyday life. Your faith isn't like some kind of watertight compartment, insulated against everything else. What you believe about God affects the way you live—your hopes, your moral standards and your general outlook on life. But this interaction is two-way. What's happening to you in your everyday life affects the quality of your faith. If you are depressed about your career or your family, if a relationship is going wrong, or if you are worried about money—then don't be surprised if these anxieties reduce your spiritual well-being.

For most people, the types of anxiety that can give rise to doubt are far more mundane than those that arise from the worlds of power politics and high finance. Let's look at some obvious examples.

It is quite common for someone already involved in a *personal relationship* to become a Christian, while the other person involved does not. This can cause enormous difficulties and tensions. In the first place, becoming a Christian involves a new interest in God, which expresses itself in certain very obvious ways—such as a new interest in reading the Bible, talking about Jesus Christ, going to church, getting involved with Christian groups and so forth. This change can be very distressing for the other party, who is probably unable to understand what has happened, let alone share in it. In the second place, it means becoming involved with a new group of people—at church, at the college or campus Christian union, or at a local home group. The other party might feel excluded from these.

It is very difficult for someone who has just become a Christian to avoid feeling the tension this change has created within the personal relationship, and it is easy then to become prone to anxiety and distress. In fact, sadly, it is quite common for the relationship to break up as a result. The tension within this relationship, while it lasts (that is, either the tension or the relationship itself), is like a thornbush, which can seriously interfere with the growth of faith and the development of Christian maturity. If you are in such a position concerning a relationship, and find doubt a problem, it is advisable to attempt to resolve the difficulties within that relationship (for example, by sharing your newfound faith and what it means to you). Perhaps the other party will feel able to accept your position—and may even eventually come to share it. However, it is necessary to inject a note of somber realism into this discussion, by pointing out that the more usual course is for the relationship to break up. So, a simple word of advice if you are not already involved in this kind of personal relationship: let your serious relationships be with other Christians!

When this happens in a student relationship, often the relationship is exploratory in nature, not necessarily leading to the permanence of marriage, so the trauma caused by the breaking up of such a relationship is not as severe as it might otherwise be. This difficulty is much more serious, of course, within a marriage, when one of the partners comes to faith, leaving the other in a state of unbelief. The tensions this can create are considerable and require handling with sensitivity and compassion. While a detailed response to this difficulty is impossible within the limited space of this work, the suggestions for further reading should prove helpful in coping with and perhaps resolving such a situation.

Some people find themselves seriously behind with their *work,* due to illness, laziness, a lack of personal discipline, or a fundamental inability to cope with a subject at school or a task at work. The pressure that work can create is considerable and may totally dominate a person's horizons. As a result of this pressure, a person can easily become swamped with work and thrown into a state of despair. All his or her resources are drawn into the struggle to keep up with task deadlines or essay assignments, with everything else being neglected in order to focus on this one objective. It is hardly surprising that God tends to get squeezed out of such situations. If this is happening to you, it is important to realize what is going on. There are ways of coping with work and the stress it causes, which you will find explored in the material suggested for further reading. Investigate these!

Problems with work sometimes arise from sheer laziness or a lack of personal discipline. These are weaknesses that can also affect your faith. If you lack discipline in work, you will probably also lack discipline in prayer and studying Scripture. If you take a laidback attitude to your work, you will probably also take the same attitude to your faith. The result is a vulnerable and superficial faith. Why not aim for a sense of personal discipline in both your work and your faith?

It is perfectly understandable that you should be anxious about *the future,* especially during life's transitions. The decisions you make can be of considerable importance in affecting your future career or your family, and they can have enormous implications for the remainder of your life. Some people feel overwhelmed by such anxieties—once more making them vulnerable to doubt. It is important that you commit such decisions to God. Ask him for guidance, for wisdom and for courage to make the right decisions. But above all, ask for peace of mind as you explore possibilities for the future. The Old Testament word for *faith* can be translated as "being strong in the Lord." Learn to trust in him, to commit the unknown future to the known care of the Lord. See yourself as being like Abraham or Joshua, setting out into the unknown future, secure in the knowledge that, wherever you go and whatever happens to you, the Lord will be with you, by your side (Genesis 12:1-2; Joshua 1:1-9). If your anxiety is about vocational guidance, there is much material available, including some suggestions at the end of this chapter, which you might find helpful.

These, then, are some of the ways in which faith can be weakened through outside factors. Remember this if you feel low or depressed and far from God. You are not immune from outside influences—in fact, all of us are highly vulnerable to them. Try to identify what it is that is making you feel anxious, and see if you can do something about it. Try to develop a sense of spiritual discipline, as suggested below, and not be unduly influenced by your circumstances.

DEVELOP SPIRITUAL DISCIPLINE

Many Christians draw back from the idea of spiritual discipline. They may suspect that it is inconsistent with the freedom of the gospel. They may view it as a lapse into some form of legalism. Actually, it's nothing of the sort. It is a means by which God may graciously deepen our faith in him, our knowledge of him and our obedience to him. It means taking God seriously enough to ensure we get to spend time with him, despite all the pressures on us. It means acknowledging that we cannot hope to keep going as Christians without the continual support of God—thus structuring our lives to allow that support to get through. This is no legalism, a routine for a routine's sake; rather, it is a sign of deepening obedience and commitment, which are the hallmarks of a maturing faith.

Suppose you take up a demanding job in a major international corporation or in a caring agency in which considerable demands are made of your time and attention. It is very easy to become so busy, so preoccupied with countless matters, that it becomes difficult to find time to spend with God. Everything else seems to get in the way. Developing a spiritual discipline means setting time aside as a matter of deliberate policy to be with God.

If you're going through a spiritual dry patch and are finding the going rough, all the pressures of work or family which come to bear on you will make it difficult for you to find time to be alone with God. Yet your growth in faith depends on being able to spend time in this way. And if you aren't able to spend time with God in prayer and adoration, you'll find that your faith becomes vulnerable. You're under pressure and won't have access to the spiritual resources to cope with it. Give God some breaks by allowing him space to draw alongside you.

By developing a spiritual discipline, you can build time into your routine to be set aside for God—and nothing or nobody else! If you can start developing a discipline like this now, you'll find that it will stay with you. What kind of times? Some prefer to set aside time early in the morning, before the day's work begins. It allows you time to commit the coming day to God and ask for his strength and guidance to face all that it will bring. Some people find it helpful to pray with their diaries open in front of them. For others, the best time is late at night, when the pressures of the day are lifted. The day's work is over, the children are asleep, the world is quiet: you can spend time reading, meditating and praying in peace. And try to keep Sunday special, despite all the pressure to work right through the weekend. If you're too busy to spend time with God, you're busier than God ever meant you to be.

The worst thing you can do in the event of a spiritual dry patch is to give up going to church, spending time with Christian friends and colleagues, or reading Scripture. These can keep you going when your prayer life seems to dry up. They are like roots, searching for precious moisture in a dry land. Jeremiah likened someone who trusts in the Lord to a tree planted by a stream (Jeremiah 17:7-8):

> Blessed are those who trust in the LORD,
>> whose trust is the LORD.
> They shall be like a tree planted by water,
>> sending out its roots by the stream.
> It shall not fear when heat comes,
>> and its leaves shall stay green;
> in the year of drought it is not anxious,
>> and it does not cease to bear fruit.

So keep your roots in place, waiting for the water to return—and return it will.

> Wait for the LORD;
>> be strong, and let your heart take courage;
>> wait for the LORD! (Psalm 27:14)

Let's look at the way spiritual discipline can help you handle doubt.

Girding your faith. First, having spiritual discipline helps make your faith less vulnerable. It builds time for reading of Scripture, for praying and for waiting on God into what can become an unbearably busy timetable. It ensures that you aren't cut off from your lifeline to God. It gives you access to vital spiritual resources, which you will need to cope with the pressures of life.

When I studied biology at school, I remember learning about

the water-spider. This little spider lives on the bottom of ponds, in a small gossamer case looking like a thimble. This case has a hole at its base through which the spider can enter. On reaching the surface of the pond, the spider entraps air bubbles by means of hooked hairs. He then dives down to the case and sets the air bubbles free inside the case. After several such trips, the spider has accumulated enough air to allow him to live in his case for some time beneath the water. Even though the environment is alien and hostile, the spider can survive—because of his air supply from the upper world. However, eventually the oxygen in that vital air supply is used up. The spider is then obliged to return to the surface and to gather more air. Without it, he cannot survive beneath the surface of the water.

As Christians, we are in a situation similar to that water-spider. We exist in a hostile environment, nourished and supported by resources from above. But our resources must be renewed and replenished—otherwise, they will run out. The spiritual life demands continual access to spiritual resources. The spider's regular journeys to the surface of the water remind us of our need for regular fellowship with God, in order that our batteries may be recharged and our resources renewed (to jumble together several helpful images). We cannot allow those resources to become dangerously low, as we do not know when we may need to draw heavily on them. Just as the foolish maidens allowed the oil supplies in their lamps to grow dangerously low (Matthew 25:1-13), obliging them to miss the opportunity of greeting the bridegroom, so we must be disciplined in maintaining our spiritual resources. You never know when you might need them—and need them badly.

Preventing panic and prompting patience. Second, it prevents you from burning your bridges (usually by accident, rather than design) if you do go through a period of doubt. Younger Christians in particular are tempted to give up praying and reading Scripture if they stop experiencing God as present in their lives. Not only can experience be an unreliable guide to the reality and presence of God, but by overreacting in this way, you make it more difficult for God to draw close to you again. The sense of expectation of God is lost. At the first sign of doubt, some young Christians panic and abandon their faith—needlessly. Soldiers learn discipline so that they will not panic at the first sight of a threat. If you have developed a sense of spiritual discipline, you will reap the rewards of patience. For Christianity is not an easy ride through life but is a struggle against sin, disobedience and doubt—all of which attempt to tear us away from God. It is a battle in which discipline adds strength to your own spiritual resources and allows you to draw increasingly on the might of God.

These, then, are some strategies both for coping with doubt and making your faith less vulnerable. Remember that a superficial faith is a vulnerable faith, just as a shallow-rooted plant is easily uprooted. So let those roots grow!

11

DOUBT

Putting It in Perspective

How can we put doubt in perspective? One very helpful way is to see how some biblical narratives help us grasp the nature of doubt, thus enabling us to deal with it more effectively. In earlier chapters we explored how doubt arose through not fully understanding the situation. Two classic examples of this are provided by the exodus of Israel from Egypt in the Old Testament and by the crucifixion of Jesus Christ in the New Testament. Reflecting on the exodus and the death of Christ puts doubt in its proper perspective. Let's see how.

DOUBT IN PERSPECTIVE—THE EXODUS FROM EGYPT

The exodus from Egypt is one of the most powerful and memorable stories the world has ever known. It tells of the liberation of the people of Israel from their bondage in Egypt. It recounts their long and difficult struggle to gain access to the Promised Land. But it also helps us understand how doubt arises and gives us some clues about how to see it in its proper perspective. Three points are of special importance about that exodus.

It means leaving behind security. "Why did we ever leave

Egypt? Things weren't so bad there!" For some of the Israelites, the realities of life as they passed from Egypt to the Promised Land were unacceptable (Numbers 11:1-20). They began to look back on their days in Egypt with something approaching nostalgia! They thought that liberation from Egyptian captivity would mean the end of all their problems. Instead, they found themselves with a new set of problems.

Some people begin the Christian life with the mistaken idea that all will be marvelous thereafter. When things get tough, they begin to doubt. Yet what we are promised in the gospel is not an easy ride through life. The Christian life is difficult and demanding. Liberation from bondage to sin and the fear of death opens up the prospect of a new life and a new lifestyle—but they are not easy options. Our responsibilities to God are demanding, and the challenges he lays before us are considerable. But we are promised that, whatever life may hold for us, God will be present to support and sustain us. I simply cannot express adequately how comforting and important that is.

It means going through a wilderness period. The people of Israel set out from Egypt in good spirits. The presence and the power of God was made clear and real through signs and wonders. God seemed very close and very real during those first days. And then the long, hard journey through the wilderness began. The going got tough. The memory of the presence and power of God faded. Signs and wonders seemed far away. Doubt and disbelief began to set in for some. Of course, the promise of the presence of God had not been canceled. Nor had the Promised Land been set to one side. But the promises seemed unreal in the wilderness situation.

Some Christians encounter the same kind of experience. They

feel that they are struggling through a spiritual wilderness. The dynamism and excitement they may have felt in the first days of faith seem to have gone forever. They are suffering from spiritual drought and famine and are unable to satisfy their needs. Doubt sets in. It is at this point that spiritual discipline becomes crucial. Keep going! Learn to make the use of the resources available in that situation. After all, the Israelites were provided with manna from heaven, to keep them going through the wilderness till they entered the Promised Land.

Look around and see what the Lord has made available to you. There are individuals you can talk to who have been through that same wilderness experience and can tell of its trials and tribulations. They can tell of the joy of leaving it behind and of the spiritual lessons they learned. There are books that you can read. But above all, see a wilderness experience as a possible time of growth—a time in which you can learn more about yourself and about God. A wilderness experience is a time of trial. Your faith is being tested and its weak points identified to you and for you.

An illustration may help make this clearer. I was born in Belfast, the capital city of Northern Ireland. One of the greatest moments in the history of that city was the launching of the White Star Liner *Titanic* in 1911. It was the greatest ship ever built, and it was destined to work the dangerous run across the Atlantic Ocean. But would it stand up to the conditions of that run? Would it survive the dangerous seas or the ice packs off the Canadian coast? In the course of its journeys across the ocean, it would encounter severe and testing conditions. Could it cope with them?

To answer this question, the *Titanic* was subjected to sea trials. In theory, they would test the ship to its limits, showing up any obvious weaknesses. Once these weaknesses could be detected, they could be put right. Then the really dangerous voyages could be undertaken. Sadly, those sea trials were not severe enough. The ship was passed as seaworthy. The cruel truth came to light when she sank on her maiden voyage in 1912 with terrible loss of life.

The Christian life is like a long and dangerous voyage, during which your resources may be tested to the full on occasion. Think of doubt as being like a sea trial, gently showing up your weaknesses. Is your faith deep enough and your trust in God strong enough? Once you know your weaknesses, you can do something about them—so that if real difficulties come your way, you'll be able to cope with them. It's all part of growing deeper in your faith (see 1 Corinthians 10:13; 1 Peter 5:10).

Doubt, then, can be a wilderness experience. If you feel you are going through this kind of experience, use it positively. Remember that Jesus himself went through a period of testing in the wilderness, as God prepared him for the great tasks awaiting him (Matthew 4:1-11). Are you being prepared for a task? The early Christians used to go into the wilderness to get away from all sources of distraction, so that they could concentrate on God. Tell God about your feelings of doubt, of loneliness or emptiness. Commit them to him. And stay close to him, giving him some breaks. Trust him. The Promised Land is still there, awaiting your entry—with God by your side.

It means trusting in the promises of God. God promised the people of Israel "a land flowing with milk and honey" (Exodus 13:5). Yet during their period of wandering in the wilderness, they knew nothing but a barren land. The Promised Land was something held out in front of them, like a carrot in front of a donkey. The thought kept them going, yet some found it too distant a hope. It was too far in the future. They wanted instant satisfaction.

They had left behind security and the comfort of the known and were being asked to keep going into the unknown, on account of the promises of God. For some, that seemed too great a risk to take. And so they doubted.

Looking back on this, we can see that they were mistaken. The final entry into the Promised Land triumphantly vindicated the faithfulness of God to his promises. But we can understand their feelings at the time. The Promised Land seemed hopelessly distant. And for some Christians, the promises of eternal life seem very far off. If this is the case for you, try to think yourself into the exodus situation. Try to imagine how difficult it must have been to trust in the promise of the land flowing with milk and honey, when all around you was nothing but wilderness. Israel spent many years wandering in that desert, wondering if there was really anything waiting for them at the end of their journey. Then turn your mind to that great moment when Israel crossed the Jordan and entered into the Promised Land. Can you see how the exodus gives us insights into our own situation? It reminds us that, even though God's promises seem far off and distant, they will still be fulfilled. And we are not left without comfort as we trust; God gives us his Holy Spirit to comfort, reassure and challenge us as we journey in faith.

DOUBT IN PERSPECTIVE—THE FIRST GOOD FRIDAY

Try to imagine what it was like for the disciples on the first Good Friday. They had given up everything to follow Jesus. Their whole reason for living centered on him. He seemed to have the answers to all their questions. Then, in front of their eyes, he was taken from them. He was to be publicly executed. We can feel an immense sense of despair as we read the Gospel accounts of the death of Jesus. Perhaps the disciples were hoping for a miracle. Certainly, there were those in the crowd of spectators who expected God to intervene. Others were more skeptical. "He trusts in God; let God deliver him now, if he wants to" (Matthew 27:43). There seemed to be no trace of God's presence or activity at Calvary. As Jesus became weaker, the disciples must have become increasingly despondent. There was no sign of God intervening to transform the situation.

Finally, Jesus died. That would probably have been the darkest moment in the lives of the disciples. They were already demoralized enough, as Peter's denial of Jesus demonstrated. Now, as they watched the scene from a distance, it must have seemed as if their entire world had collapsed, shown up as a fraud and an illusion. What sorts of thoughts might have gone through their minds? Perhaps that Jesus was no different from any other man? Perhaps that God was not there—or that if he was, he showed no interest whatsoever in the fate of Jesus?

Of course, we know the outcome of that story too. We know how the disciples' sorrow was transformed to joy and wonder as the news of the resurrection of Jesus became known. The theme of the resurrection of the crucified Christ pervades the writings of Paul and provides the standpoint from which he interprets the crucifixion. The cross is not seen as a dead end but as a crucial stage on the road to resurrection and glorification. When we read the Gospel accounts of the suffering and death of Jesus, we cannot help but think ahead to his resurrection. We know that there is a happy ending to this apparent tragedy.

Now try and imagine yourself standing among the disciples as they watched Jesus suffer and die—without knowing that he would be raised again from the dead. Set aside your knowledge of what happens later, and try to imagine what it must have been like to watch Jesus die on the cross. His suffering seemed utterly pointless. What could be achieved through it? And where was God in all this? Why didn't he intervene? It was all enough to make anyone doubt whether God existed in the first place. And if he did exist, he seemed to be totally indifferent to the sufferings of Jesus. What hope was there for anyone else if God treated Jesus this way? It is easy to get a feel for the sense of despair and bewilderment on that sad day.

All those doubts were resolved through the resurrection. The apparently pointless suffering of Jesus was revealed as the means through which God atoned and provided salvation for sinful humanity. God was not absent from that scene; he was working to transform it from a scene of hopelessness and helplessness to one of joy and hope. God's love was demonstrated, not contradicted, by the death of his son (John 3:16; Romans 5:8). The resurrection transformed the disciple's understanding of the way in which God was present and active in his world.

Let's apply this model, and see what insights it affords.

Our feelings of God's presence can be unreliable. Jesus' death brings home to us how unreliable experience and feelings can be as guides to the presence of God. Those around the cross didn't experience the presence of God—so they concluded that he was absent from the scene. The resurrection overturns that judgment. God was present in a hidden manner, which experience mistook for his absence. Do you feel that God is absent from your life or from certain difficult situations? Are you bewildered by events or in despair over the way things are going? Then think of the first Good Friday when God also seemed to be absent—only to be shown to have been working in a hidden and mysterious way to transform it in a totally unexpected manner.

The promise of resurrection was there: Jesus had assured his disciples that he would be raised to life on the third day after his crucifixion (Matthew 20:17-19). Yet, in the desperation of that crucial moment, that promise had been forgotten—perhaps even doubted. Experience seemed to suggest it could not be fulfilled. The first Good Friday reminds us of the need to trust in the divine promises made to us, rather than rely on our feelings and experience.

Our suffering has meaning, though now mysterious. Christ's death allows us insights into the mystery of human suffering. Without knowledge of the resurrection, the sufferings of Christ seemed pointless and meaningless. With the knowledge of the resurrection, and the inestimable benefits of salvation and forgiveness that flow from it, those sufferings are seen in a new light. He suffered for us so that, through his suffering, our sin might be forgiven and our human natures healed. "He took up our infirmities / and carried our sorrows. . . . / He was pierced for our transgressions" (Isaiah 53:4-5 NIV).

This theme is developed in many ways in the New Testament. Perhaps its bearing on the suffering of believers is of most relevance to this discussion. For Paul, Christians are those who are heirs of God by adoption (Ephesians 1:4-5; cf. Romans 8:12-21). They are entitled to receive from God the same inheritance as his own Son, Jesus Christ. What is that inheritance? As the cross and resurrection make clear, the inheritance of the believer is glory gained through suffering. "We suffer with him so that we may also be glorified with him" (Romans 8:17). Suffering is thus seen as a sign of faith, a token of the glory that is to come. It is not something that can be bypassed.

Seeing the whole picture. Thinking of the first Good Friday, then, helps us put our doubt in context. It allows us to see it in a new and proper perspective. We learn to see our own situation, our own doubts, our own anxieties, as being like that scene at Calvary. People asked questions that could not be answered; they voiced doubts that could not be silenced. It seemed difficult to trust God. Yet those questions and doubts were seen in a new light after the resurrection of Jesus Christ. God surprised everybody, as far as we can see, on that first Easter Day. It is this model which provides a key to our own questions, doubts and anxieties.

Doubt partly arises because of our inability to see the whole picture, to understand how the various elements of our experience interlock. Just as faith sees the crucifixion in terms of the resurrection, so we must view the perplexities of the world in the light of its future transformation into the New Jerusalem (Revelation 21:1-5). The hopelessness and helplessness of Good Friday are given new meaning in the light of Easter Day, just as the ambiguities and suffering of the present day will be seen in a new light when God brings history to its end. Good Friday and Easter Day are a model for understanding the way God is present in and at work in his world: just as Good Friday is given its meaning through Easter Day, so the pain and problems of the present day will be given new meaning at the end of time.

The doubt of Good Friday gives way to the faith of Easter Day. We do not fully understand how God is working out his purposes for the world and for us; what we do know is that God affirms, in both word and in deed, his utter faithfulness to us. He is one in whom we can trust. "Cast all your anxiety on him, because he cares for you" (1 Peter 5:7). If we cannot trust God, who can we trust?

Perhaps some will suggest we should rely on our own perception of the situation, which seems to raise difficulties for faith. But,
as the events of Calvary indicate, our perceptions of the situation
can be hopelessly misleading and inaccurate. Our perception is at
best a partial perception; we do not have access to all the data we
require in order to make an informed analysis of the situation. God
was perceived to be absent from the crucifixion—until the resurrection demonstrated him to have been present, secretly working
out the redemption of humanity and the glorification of his Son.

Perhaps others might suggest that we rely on our feelings and
emotions. If God isn't felt as real, he isn't real, they might suggest.
If we don't experience him as present, he isn't present. But how
unreliable our feelings can be here! They are influenced by a huge
variety of factors: our health, the weather, the state of our bank
balance, our personal relationships, our work or career—just to
name the more obvious ones! God doesn't cease to exist just because we've had a bad day at the office or had an argument with a
friend. Our emotions, distracted and confused by our various anxieties, may tell us that God isn't here—but that is not a particularly
reliable or informed judgment.

In the end, Christianity stands or falls with the trustworthiness
and reliability of the God who raised Jesus Christ from the dead.
By meditating on that first Good Friday, we can remind ourselves
of the unreliability of our own judgment, on the one hand, and of
the faithfulness of God to his promises on the other—thus we can
put doubt in its proper perspective. For, seen properly, doubt is
not a threat to faith but a reminder of how fragile a hold we have
on our knowledge of God—and how gracious God is in having revealed himself to us. For, without God's revelation of himself, we
would have been left totally in the dark concerning him and his

love for us. God is not capricious or whimsical, nor does he fail to stand by his promises or to act in accordance with his nature and character, as we know it through Scripture and through Jesus Christ. Instead, we know a God who is faithful to his covenant, who promises mercy and forgiveness to those who put their trust in him. Instead of trusting in our own perception of a situation, or relying on our feelings and emotions, we should learn to trust in the faithfulness and constancy of God.

THE IMPORTANCE OF APOLOGETICS

Finally, I need to stress the importance of the Christian discipleship of the mind. *Apologetics* is basically about being able to give answers to people who want to know more about Christianity. "Always be ready to make your defense to anyone who demands from you an accounting for the hope that is in you" (1 Peter 3.15). Sometimes, these questions are about problems that people have with faith—for example, the presence of suffering in the world or the difficulty accepting that Jesus is indeed the Son of God. With others, the questions are about the relevance of the gospel. Why is the gospel good news? How does it affect me? As Christians, we ought to be able to give answers to these questions. It is essential to effective evangelism.

But apologetics is important for another reason. It will certainly equip you to answer your friends' questions. *But it will also help you answer your own questions.* Apologetics is not only about engaging with the questions that our culture is asking. It is about engaging with the questions that linger within our own souls. I would urge you as readers to take the time to undertake this "discipleship of the mind." Before you can answer the questions about faith raised by the world, you need to answer them for yourself. And there are

answers to be found—answers in abundance, which will sometimes reassure you, sometimes challenge you and sometimes excite you.

For Christians, apologetics can be thought of as functioning in
two quite different ways, which we could described as objective
and subjective. *Objectively,* apologetics reassures those inside the
church of the credentials of the Christian faith. It aims to reassure
Christian believers of the reliability of the Gospels, the reality of
the death and resurrection of Christ, and the interpretation of
these events in Christian doctrines—such as the divinity of Christ.
It provides us with answers to some of the questions that we struggle with and, thus, enables us to resolve these issues. And that
means we are much better equipped to handle those same questions when asked by seekers.

And *subjectively,* apologetics creates a climate of intellectual
confidence. By this I do not mean arrogance or complacency but
a quiet confidence that the Christian faith is, in the first place, true,
and that in the second, it really works. This means that believers
come to "feel good" about their faith—not so much individual aspects of that faith but faith in its broad totality. Apologetics builds
up confidence in the total package of the Christian gospel and creates an atmosphere of confidence within the church—a climate of
confidence that, in turn, nourishes evangelism and church
growth. So apologetics both nourishes the faith of believers and
encourages outreach to those beyond the church.

So may I leave you with a challenge? Discover why Christians
believe in the Trinity. Or the divinity of Jesus Christ. Why? To reassure yourself of their truth and their relevance. I have only mentioned two areas of faith; you can easily add to this. Remember my
argument throughout this book: doubt is often a symptom of a

faith that needs to grow—to put down deeper roots. Studying apologetics is one way of nourishing your mind and strengthening your faith. It will help you to grow in faith—and to answer those questions that your friends will want to ask you.

CONCLUSION

Doubt is a subject that many Christians find both difficult and sensitive. They may see it as something shameful and disloyal, on the same level as heresy. As a result, it is often something that they don't—or won't—talk about. They suppress it. Others fall into the opposite trap—they get totally preoccupied by doubt. They get overwhelmed by it. They lose sight of God through concentrating on themselves. Yet doubt is something too important to be treated in either of these ways. Viewed positively, doubt provides opportunities for spiritual growth. It tests your faith and shows you where it is vulnerable. It forces you to think about your faith and not just take it for granted. It stimulates you to strengthen the foundations of your relationship with God.

I hope that this book will not just help you to handle doubts, but will allow you to begin evolving strategies for spiritual discipline and growth, developing both the personal and doctrinal aspects of your faith. Viewed positively, doubt can be a way to rediscovering the full depths of faith and growing in your commitment to the gospel. It is a constant reminder that we need to discover more of this God who has called us, who invites us to know him more fully and deeply. Be reassured that "the one who calls you is faithful, and he will do this" (1 Thessalonians 5:24).

FOR FURTHER STUDY

You will find a wide range of resources—including book lists, articles, recordings of talks and presentations—at the Ravi Zacharias International Ministry website, which I strongly recommended as a resource, especially in the area of Christian apologetics: <www.rzim.org>.

This website provides access to articles, addresses and reading lists that you may find helpful, as well as connects you with events organized by this major, highly respected international ministry.

The additional works, which follow, will help you follow up on some of the issues discussed in this book.

Boot, Joe. *Searching for Truth: Discovering the Meaning and Purpose of Life*. Wheaton, Ill.: Crossway Books, 2003.

Evans, C. Stephen. *Quest for Faith*. Downers Grove, Ill.: InterVarsity Press, 1986.

Green, Michael. *Avoiding Jesus: Answers for Skeptics, Cynics and the Curious*. Grand Rapids: Baker, 2005.

Guinness, Os. *God in the Dark: The Assurance of Faith Beyond a Shadow of Doubt*. Wheaton, Ill.: Crossway Books, 1996.

———. *Time for Truth: Living Free in a World of Lies, Hype & Spin*. Grand Rapids: Baker, 2000.

Holmes, Arthur F. *Faith Seeks Understanding.* Grand Rapids: Eerd-
    mans, 1971.

Kreeft, Peter. *Fundamentals of the Faith: Essays in Christian Apologet-
    ics.* San Francisco: Ignatius Press, 1988.

————. *Making Sense Out of Suffering.* New York: Phoenix Press,
    1986.

Kreeft, Peter, and Ronald K. Tacelli. *Handbook of Christian Apolo-
    getics.* Downers Grove, Ill.: InterVarsity Press, 1994.

Lewis, C. S. *The Problem of Pain.* San Francisco: HarperSanFran-
    cisco, 2001.

————. *Surprised by Joy.* New York: Harcourt Brace, 1955.

McGrath, Alister E. *Intellectuals Don't Need God and Other Modern
    Myths.* Grand Rapids: Zondervan, 1993.

————. *The Twilight of Atheism: The Rise and Fall of Unbelief in the
    Modern World.* New York: Doubleday, 2003.

Medawar, Peter B. *The Limits of Science.* Oxford: Oxford University
    Press, 1985.

Mitchell, Basil. *The Justification of Religious Belief.* Oxford: Oxford
    University Press, 1981.

Nash, Ronald. *Without a Doubt: Answering the 20 Toughest Faith
    Questions.* Grand Rapids: Baker, 2004.

Newbigin, Lesslie. *Proper Confidence: Faith, Doubt and Certainty in
    Christian Discipleship.* London: SPCK, 1995.

Orr-Ewing, Amy. *Is the Bible Intolerant?* Downers Grove, Ill.: Inter-
    Varsity Press, 2006.

Polkinghorne, John. *The Way the World Is.* London: SPCK, 1983.

Sire, James W. *The Universe Next Door.* Downers Grove, Ill.: Inter-
    Varsity Press, 2004.

————. *Why Should Anyone Believe Anything at All?* Downers
    Grove, Ill.: InterVarsity Press, 1994.

Stackhouse, John. *Humble Apologetics: Defending the Faith Today.* New York: Oxford University Press, 2002.

Tomlin, Graham. *The Provocative Church.* London: SPCK, 2002.

Witherington, Ben, III. *The Gospel Code: Novel Claims About Jesus, Mary Magdalene and Da Vinci.* Downers Grove, Ill.: InterVarsity Press, 2004.

Yancey, Philip. *Where Is God When It Hurts?* Grand Rapids: Zondervan, 1997.

———. *Reaching for the Invisible God.* Grand Rapids: Zondervan, 2000.

Zacharias, Ravi. *Can Man Live Without God?* Nashville: W Publishing Group, 1996.

ZACHARIAS TRUST

The Zacharias Trust
is the European office of
Ravi Zacharias International Ministries (RZIM).

Ravi Zacharias International Ministries seeks to reach and challenge those who shape the ideas of a culture with the credibility and the beauty of the gospel of Jesus Christ. With a team of individuals based in six countries, RZIM is committed to reaching this generation around the world— in the university, the arts, politics, business, and the church. Through open forums, community outreach, and various media, RZIM seeks to remove the barriers to the cross for the skeptic and prepare Christians to give a reason for the hope within us.

www.zactrust.org

www.rzim.org